The battle for
KINDER SCOUT

including the 1932 Mass Trespass
by BENNY ROTHMAN

The battle for
KINDER SCOUT
including the 1932 Mass Trespass
by BENNY ROTHMAN

With contributions by
ROLY SMITH, TOM WAGHORN
& KEITH WARRENDER

FOREWORD BY MIKE HARDING

Willow
PUBLISHING

First published as 'The 1932 Kinder Trespass' in 1982

Text copyright © Mike Harding 2012, © Benny Rothman 2012,
© Roly Smith 2012, © Tom Waghorn 2012,
© Keith Warrender 2012, © John Watson 2012

Benny Rothman's account has been abridged, with additions from
his interview with Graham Atkinson for the 'Socialist Worker' in 1978,
by kind permission of the Rothman family

Photographs © Keith Warrender 2012 and © Willow Publishing 2012
unless acknowledged
This edition first published 2012 by Willow Publishing

Willow Publishing, 36 Moss Lane, Timperley
Altrincham, Cheshire WA15 6SZ

ISBN 978-0-946361-44-1

Book designed by Keith Warrender
Printed by the Buxton Press

*Dedicated to the memory of those who took part
in the 1932 Kinder Scout Mass Trespass*

Cover: William Clough
Opposite title page: Kinder from the reservoir
Title page: The trespassers setting off from Hayfield

Contents

*Benny Rothman with Mike Harding at a
water privatisation rally at Hayfield, 1989*

1932 BWSP camp at Rowarth

Veterans of the 1932 trespass at the 1988 anniversary celebrations

Foreword
by MIKE HARDING

Working class heroes

The Kinder Mass Trespass was, to many of us walkers and folk singers of the 1960s and 1970s, not just some vague historical blip on the charts that had produced a reaction in the press and the imprisonment of five innocent men, which had then been lost in the clamour of the Second World War.

It was a symbol, not just of the struggle for access to the mountains, but of the whole working-class struggle for greater things: for a National Health Service, for the common ownership of infrastructure like the railways and the mines and the other things that were absolutely necessary for the wellbeing of a sane and civilised society.

Not everybody would agree with me - I know - but many of us did see the Kinder Trespass as one of the first moves towards claiming back what was the common people's by right.

I don't know what Benny and all the other young lads and lasses who took part in the Mass Trespass would make of the present stripping-back of all that we have gained in the last 70 years. But I expect that, were he alive and fit, he would still be out there fighting, and fighting hard to overturn the vandalism of the last 30-odd years.

I had the great privilege of knowing Benny and of spending time in his company; he was a wonderful man, funny and forthright with an encyclopaedic knowledge of the history of rambling and the struggle for access. I was honoured to count him as a friend and I cherish the memory of a remarkable character.

What is written here in this book will keep the flame alive - alive for another 80 years I hope. The story of the Mass Trespass and the poverty and oppression that it came out of must never be forgotten because, as a wiser man than me once said *'When the past no longer illuminates the future, the spirit walks in darkness.'* (Alexis de Tocqueville).

7

The 1932 Kinder Scout Mass Trespass

By BENNY ROTHMAN

With the passing of time, the dulling of memories and the deaths of those who took part in the trespass, a whole mythology has grown around the incident.

I believe that the Mass Trespass is too important to be dismissed either as youthful folly, or as a political stunt

The purpose of the book is to impress on outdoor lovers that access such as we have was not easily attained. It should help in making us more vigilant and determined to oppose any threat to the countryside from whatever source it might come.

Overleaf: The moor where the confrontation with the keepers took place

KEITH WARRENDER

MANCHESTER LIBRARIES & ARCHIVES

BENNY ROTHMAN

MIKE HARDING

Housing in Hulme, Manchester in the 1930s

CHAPTER ONE

Living for the Weekends

We scrambled up the steep bank off William Clough and onto the moor. Hundreds of ramblers on the Mass Trespass shook hands and congratulated each other. We had overcome the first hurdle. We were standing on forbidden land, tantalising glimpses of which we had seen from time to time in rambles along the well-trodden paths around Kinder.

Today, anybody with a good pair of legs can go on Kinder at most times of the year, apart from a few days when fire risks cause the moorland to be closed. In 1932 this was not possible. The 15 square miles of Kinder, although encircled by paths, were not crossed by a single public foot-path. Kinder contained spots of outstanding interest and rugged beauty and was a challenge to every rambler.

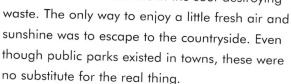

Red grouse

It is not remarkable that the Mass Trespass of 1932 happened. The trespassers were attacking the injustice of the Enclosure Acts, imposed on the public a century earlier, which confiscated common land and handed it in parcels to landowners. At the time of the original enclosures the landowners' main interest was sheeprearing. For many years it was used for the business of grouse shooting, the sport of a tiny section of wealthy people.

1932 was a grim year in Britain. Unemployment had reached peak proportions and particularly hard hit were the big industrial areas of Lancashire and Yorkshire. Manchester, Salford, Sheffield and the dozens of smaller towns and villages in the counties were deserts of bricks, mortar and cobble-stones. Living conditions were desperately bad with bug-ridden and verminous houses. Not many had gardens, there were very few trees, shrubs or flowers in the soul-destroying waste. The only way to enjoy a little fresh air and sunshine was to escape to the countryside. Even though public parks existed in towns, these were no substitute for the real thing.

Rambling and cycling were mass sports. Cars were too expensive for most people. The railway companies competed for the custom of ramblers. Rambling clubs and federations and associations, together with railway companies, organised special rail tickets for walkers. Tea-rooms and cheap cafes catered for the thousands of ramblers and

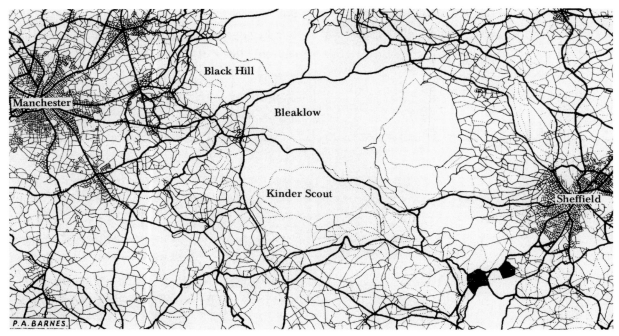

Map in The 1934 'Trespassers will be Prosecuted' showing the lack of public footpaths crossing Kinder and Bleaklow.

cyclists who poured into the countryside every weekend. Most newspapers had a rambling column. Special rambles led by experienced walkers were regularly advertised in local newspapers and ramblers' excursions were put on by railway companies. Town dwellers lived for weekends when they could go camping in the country, while unemployed young people would return home just to 'sign on' at the labour exchanges and collect their dole money. Rambling, cycling and camping clubs grew in membership.

A feature of Sunday mornings was the cycling clubs strung out along the country lanes and roads. Cycling clubhouses were packed on Sunday evenings when clubs met after their day's outing for a sing-song and dance - not only young bloods on racing bikes, but husbands and wives on tandems, and grandads and grandmas riding their light-weight bikes. The Sunday morning queues of ramblers on Manchester's London Road (Piccadilly) Station stretched down the station approaches. The platforms rang to the sound of nailed boots - rubber and Vibram soles had not yet been invented. Most working-class ramblers wore ex-army boots which they nailed themselves, and often they wore them at work to break them in. Rambling gear was very varied. Shorts were usually worn by both the lads and

girls, together with coloured shirts, sweaters and often ex-army jackets. More sober knee-breeches and woollen jackets were reserved for 'posh' rambling clubs. Anoraks were unknown in Britain.

Camping too was more free and easy and rough and ready. The regulations on camping, restricting it to licensed sites only, had not yet come into existence. Tents were only of the bivouac type. The sophisticated canvas homes, now so popular, were not then available. Camp fires, dixies and Primus stoves were the only way to cook meals.

But despite the apparent inconvenience compared with today's standards, weekends in the country made life worth living.

Weekend and holiday camps in the country grew year by year, both in numbers and in popularity. Young people were escaping from the squalor and monotony of the towns on bikes and on foot, but as the numbers of cyclists and ramblers grew new problems arose. The popular footpaths of the Peak District soon became morasses and quagmires in wet weather. The feeling of being close to nature receded as the crowds grew, and ramblers looked longingly at the acres of empty peat bogs, moorlands and the tops, which were forbidden territory.

Top: Kinder Downfall

Left: 'Ramblers Special' arriving at Hayfield, although some of the passengers were only dressed for the nearby tea rooms

STOCKPORT ARCHIVES

The high moorland areas were guarded by gamekeepers armed with sticks, which some were not afraid to use against solitary walkers. The more adventurous ramblers, when and where they could, would break off the footpaths onto the private land, but the wily gamekeepers watching through telescopes from hiding places would try to head them off. Some of the more unreasonable keepers, instead of escorting ramblers to the nearest footpath, would force them to walk miles out of their way, causing them to miss their train connections. Very often a keeper would provoke a scuffle with a rambler who would be given a beating, but there were occasions when the rambler

'Grossly abused'

A Manchester Guardian letter written in 1872 highlighted the keepers' robust response towards anyone trespassing on Kinder. The correspondent described how his party were stopped by two keepers as they walked towards Kinder. They noticed there was a group of ramblers already on the plateau.

When they re-tried to walk to the plateau, the keepers released two dogs on them. Although the dogs did not touch them, they leapt at them and barked fiercely. Two of the group were hit by the keepers with sticks and they were forced back down the hillside. They later learned that the group picnicking on Kinder had obtained permission from the landowner. The letter to the newspaper was to warn the 'innocent and unwary traveller' that if found they would be 'abused most grossly'.

would administer one to the keeper. In theory it was possible to obtain permission from landowners to ramble on moorland. In practice it was very difficult. Since 1884 attempts had been made for an Access to Mountains Bill to be presented in Parliament to give the Public the unrestricted right to walk on uncultivated moorland. The hopes of such an Act being passed seemed to recede as the years passed by. Some Members of Parliament expressed their sympathy and support. Liberal newspapers railed at the injustice of the situation. Mass demonstrations of ramblers were held, but the landowning lobby was too powerful.

Access to Mountains demonstration at The Winnats, June 1929

Above: An earlier success of the Peak and Northern Footpaths Society - opening of the Snake Path west of the Kinder plateau

Left: An early postcard view of a frozen Kinder Downfall

Below inset: James Watts

Prepared to go to prison

In August 1894, a large crowd of ramblers gathered in expectation of crossing the Kinder plateau. However, the organizing committee decided the action would be illegal and instead, held a meeting in Hayfield. One of the speakers, WH Chadwick, outlined the case for the right of people to walk over the once common land. To great applause, he said that he was prepared to walk across Kinder even if it meant imprisonment. While this action was not carried out, it was agreed to press for the re-opening of the old Hayfield footpath to the Snake over the lower slopes of Kinder.   (KW)

S. & J. WATTS & Cº

JAMES WATTS.
HUMPHREY WATTS.
HENRY LYONEL WATTS.
JAMES WATTS JUN.

MANCHESTER.

Telegraphic Address: "**WATTSES**"

It has been my practice of late to allow members of the public, who asked for such permission, to walk over my portion of Kinder Scout, when I could do so without detriment to the value of the ground as a grouse moor.

Applications have, however, become so numerous, that as a result of trying to give permission as much as possible, the Downfall area is now completely deserted by grouse, which will not stay on ground which is continually disturbed.

As I am still taxed and rated on the sporting value of this ground as if it still existed, I trust that those who apply will not think me unreasonable if I am compelled to refuse permission and try to recreate the value on which I am made to pay.

JAMES WATTS.

KINDER SCOUT TRESPASSES

£5 REWARD

will be paid for the name, address and occupation of any of the persons represented in the photos.

Apply:—COBBETT, WHEELER & COBBETT, Solicitors,
49, Spring Gardens. —————————————————Manchester.

The notorious reward notice which appeared in the Manchester Evening Chronicle in 1923 which attempted to identify trespassers. The notice provoked such an outcry it was never used again.

By 1932 the Access to Mountains Act was as far away as ever. It was in this situation that the British Workers' Sports Federation began to organise open-air activity in the North.

Previously, the federation had been mainly London-based. It was started in 1928 essentially as a working-class movement to organise sport for workers.

In the Manchester area it held its first camp at Easter 1930 at Disley. From then on it organised weekend, Easter and Whit week camps at Marple, Rowarth and Little Hayfield, so introducing many young people to the countryside. Inevitably, the favourite events were the organised rambles, and it was arising from such a ramble at our Rowarth camp at Easter 1932 that the idea of the Mass Trespass originated.

The ramblers had intended to go on to Bleaklow, but the small band of about nine was stopped at Yellowslacks by a group of gamekeepers. They were abused, threatened and turned back. To add to the humiliation of the Manchester ramblers, a number of those present were from the London BWSF, and were astounded by the incident. There were not enough ramblers to force their way through, so, crestfallen, they had to return to camp without the Londoners seeing the wildness of Bleaklow with its groughs and peatbogs. Back at camp, it was agreed that if enough ramblers had been there, no body of keepers could have kept them off the moorland. We decided to organise a Mass Trespass to prove our point.

Lance Helman and friends at a BWSF camp at Rowarth

After the camp, the Manchester area committee, with representatives from Manchester, Eccles, Salford, Swinton and Stockport, met and decided on a Mass Trespass on to Kinder Scout. Why Kinder? Because this was the outstanding stretch of moorland uncrossed by even a single footpath; its rugged tops could be seen from many points on the public footpaths and roads around, and it was the forbidden territory most known to the hundreds of ramblers travelling from Hayfield, Glossop, Chinley and Edale.

Top: Rowarth BWSF Camp 1932, Benny Rothman is end right of the second row.

Left: Disley Camp, Benny is second left on the front row.

Benny had been camping, cycling and rambling with workmates at weekends since around 1925. He then got involved in running BWSF camps using ex-army equipment and an old marquee. Some of the people who came did not even have a sleeping bag or blanket. Nevertheless the campers enjoyed themselves in all weathers with rambles and sing-songs around the campfire. It was one of Benny's jobs to keep the sexes apart because the local authority would have closed the camp if they found anything untoward in behaviour or in the general cleanliness of the site.

17

Right: Benny aged 15 on his first camping trip at Knott End near Fleetwood. This was his first bike made from old spares for £4 and paid for by his grandmother. There is an old school satchel on the handlebars and he is wearing school socks. He slept in a shed sharing it with a goat and her two kids.

Benny Rothman, cyclist, naturalist and rambler

Opposite: Phil Barnes' impressive 1934 book which was part of the campaign for greater access to the moorland of the Peak District. It contained a photo of the Kinder Mass Trespass as well as many photographs of areas forbidden to the ramblers.

CHAPTER TWO

Opposition

The decision to organise a Mass Trespass was taken and publicity for the event started immediately. As the secretary of the Lancashire BWSF, I visited the Manchester Evening Chronicle and gave an interview on the proposed trespass. The paper prominently published the interview, embellishing it by saying that the BWSF was proposing to throw hundreds of 'shock troops' on to Kinder. (This was in 1932 before Hitler's shocktroops had even been heard of outside Germany.)

The reaction in the rambling world was instantaneous. The Manchester Ramblers' Federation was hostile to the Trespass. Prominent ramblers' leaders prophesied dire consequences if the Mass Trespass took place, one saying that it would put back access to mountains by 40 years and antagonise the landowners. But in Sheffield, where the rambling movement was at a more grass roots level, they were not so antagonistic. Most newspapers were hostile and letters of opposition appeared in the correspondence columns during the following week. In addition we published duplicated leaflets and handed them out to ramblers at the station during the weekend prior to the Trespass. These were generally well received.

We announced a ramblers' meeting at the Hayfield recreation ground for Sunday, April 24, commencing at 2pm, followed by a Mass

DIRECT ACTION BY RAMBLERS.

"MASS TRESPASS" ON KINDER SCOUT

TO ENFORCE ACCESS CLAIMS.

Three hundred ramblers belonging to working-class organisations will advance on Kinder Scout, Derbyshire, on Sunday next to enforce their claims for free access to the beauty spots of the countryside.

This method of mass trespasses on disputed territory has been devised by the Lancashire district of the British Workers' Sports Federation, who are asking all clubs affiliated with them to meet at Hayfield on Sunday, from which spot the advance will be made.

The ramblers state they are "tired of unproductive protests and pleas" and they hope by this new method to force landowners to concede them the right to ramble over their property.

There is no public footpath over Kinder, a fact which the ramblers regard as an injustice.

PROTESTS INEFFECTIVE.

"We are pinning our faith in this method," Mr. B. Rothman, secretary of the Lancashire district of the British Workers' Sports Federation stated to-day.

"All of the fifteen clubs in Lancashire affiliated to our organisation will be represented at the rally, and they will be augmented by two of our Sheffield clubs.

"With sufficient support we believe we can make our action effective, even in face of the opposition we shall no doubt receive from gamekeepers and police.

"We feel we cannot any longer submit to being deprived of the beauties of the countryside for the convenience of the landowners.

"Wherever we claim we have a just right to go we shall trespass en masse. And Sunday will be but the opening our our campaign."

Manchester Evening Chronicle

Trespass over Kinder. We decided on a speaker, I was to act as chairman, and we appointed stewards for both the meeting and the Trespass. We did not announce or even plan the route: that was to be decided on the day. This was not a clever tactic on our part, it was sheer inexperience. However, we were fully convinced of the justice of our cause and felt that this was sufficient to ensure success. For the next few days the arguments for and against the Mass Trespass raged in the newspaper columns.

land, and were also beginning to go abroad where access problems did not arise.

We doubted that they wanted us on the moors any more than did the landowners, and they appeared to be quite happy with the existing state of affairs.

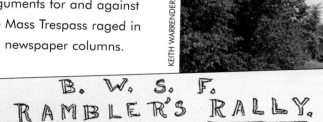
KEITH WARRENDER

Above: Hayfield Recreation Ground today
Left: Flyer circulated around Eccles

To add to the problems there was a very big age gap between us. We were very young, almost

One of our problems was that the BWSF was not an integral part of the Ramblers' Federation. We were newcomers to rambling. In addition, we were essentially a working-class movement and most of the established rambling clubs consisted of either middle-class professional people, or specialist ramblers such as ornithologists, botanists and geologists. They were highly suspicious of us and we were frankly suspicious of them. They believed that we were 'politically motivated' and loutish. We knew that many of the more exclusive clubs were occasionally obtaining permits to go on to the moor-

entirely under 21. The established rambling clubs were of a far older age group, and had spent a lifetime in the rambling movement. We were impatient at the seemingly futile efforts so far made to achieve access to mountains. Conditions in towns were becoming more intolerable and unemployment, which stood at about four million, greatly added to our frustration. We believed that we could achieve a breakthrough. The patronising opposition of many rambling organisation leaders and the downright hostility of the landowners' lobby, only strengthened our determination.

The response to the planned trespass ...

PEAK TRESPASS PROTESTS.

MOB LAW ON THE MOORS.

DAMAGING EFFECT OF "MASS TRESPASS."

RAMBLERS OBJECT TO DRASTIC MOVE.

Much of the sympathy and influence which have been enlisted in support of the Access to Mountains Bill, which, it is hoped, will eventually become law, is likely the "Evening Chronicle" is able to state, to be alienated if the proposal of a Manchester rambling organisation to organise a "mass trespass" on Kinder Scout on Sunday is persisted in.

This method of enforcing claims for free access to beauty spots" has been devised by the Lancashire district of the British Workers' Sports Federation, but it commands no support from the scores of other rambling organisations which exist in the Manchester district.

The danger of "mob law" usurping constitutional methods in the ventilation of grievances, real or imagined, is viewed with apprehension not only by landowners, but by thousands of ramblers.

PRIVILEGES APPRECIATED.

It is pointed out that the general body of ramblers are keenly appreciative of the privileges they enjoy by the good grace of landowners in the Peak District, and the prospect of facing a brush with the police in the attempt to enforce a claim, which

would at best be of doubtful benefit, is abhorrent to most of them.

The view is generally held that trespass on land which costs considerable sums to maintain, and which provides employment for a considerable number of people, is indefensible.

DOING NO SERVICE.

"Those who trespass, however well-meaning they may be, will do the rambling movement no service," said a well-known Manchester rambling official to the *Evening Chronicle* to-day.

"There are many paths which are open to all ramblers, and practically all the best country is crossed by such public paths. In cases where paths are wrongfully closed the Footpaths Society takes the matter up.

"But where there are no such paths ramblers are better advised if they apply to the proprietors for permission before walking over the land.

"Those who organise these trespasses should take care that they do not allow themselves to be confused with hooligan elements who do wilful damage.

"They would be wiser to devote their energies to supporting the movement of the Ramblers' Federation and other open-air bodies in favour of the Access to Mountains Bill, the object of which is to secure the same rights for ramblers, but by legal means.'

"Kinder, he added, was particularly unsuitable for such activity, in view of the danger to ramblers who became detached from the main body."

'The view is generally held that trespass on land which costs considerable sums to maintain, and which provides employment for a considerable number of people, is indefensible.'

'Trespassing is done best alone, or with one or two companions. When you do it with a crowd all the fun goes out of it.'

'At present ramblers have the sympathy of the public in their efforts to win more facilities. We would not like to see them risk losing that support by unnecessarily provoking measures.'

Ramblers Speak Out.

To THE EDITOR OF THE EVENING CHRONICLE

SIR,—In view of the publicity which has been given to the proposed mass trespass on Kinder on Sunday next, we wish to record our protest against such a method, which we consider can only ultimately prejudice the objects which the orderly rambler has at heart.

We wish also to state that the Ramblers' Federation (Manchester and District) have no connection with the organisation which proposes this trespass.—N. WILLINGTON, General Secretary.

On Trespassing.

As an inveterate trespasser, the idea of a "mass trespass" on Kinder Scout, which, I see, is planned for Sunday, does not appeal to me.

That may sound odd, but I always think the essence of trespassing is that it should be done quietly, neatly, and successfully.

Trespassing is done best alone, or with one or at the most two companions. When you do it with a crowd all the fun goes out of it. And there is fun in it—a sort of adult substitute for the pleasure which every youngster gets in raiding an orchard.

Making the Most of It.

If you get away with it you have done no harm (or at least I hope you haven't), and if you don't escape detection you may achieve even more.

The tactful trespasser who is stopped by farmers or gamekeepers (the latter are usually more difficult to manage) can very often make a friend for life.

I have met one or two of the pleasantest people I know while trespassing on their land. I will not attempt to explain how it is done. Everything depends on realising what sort of a man you are dealing with and your own skill. If you have enough of it, you may be asked to come again and so win rights of way and privileges that can never be secured by Act of Parliament or public demonstrations.

Ramblers' Ways.

THE Lancashire ramblers who have planned a "mass trespass" in Derbyshire next Sunday surely overstate their case when they declare they cannot submit to being "deprived of the beauties of the countryside for the convenience of landowners." "Trespassers will be prosecuted" is still far too common a notice in this country, but most of the districts worth the tramper's attention are fairly well supplied with footpaths—even if some of them are metaphorically hedged by conditions.

CERTAINLY legislation to help the rambler and country-lover moves slowly in this country—how many years is it since the Access to Mountains Bill was first thought of?—and the filching of public footpaths still goes on. But ramblers must remember that "mass trespass" is a two-edged sword and one that is more likely to provoke the withdrawal of privileges granted by private owners than to extend them.

AT present ramblers have the sympathy of the public in their efforts to win more facilities. We would not like to see them risk losing that support by unnecessarily provoking measures. There are sufficient ramblers in this country to make Parliament listen to them if they will organise themselves properly. A determined badgering of M.P.s on the lines recently adopted by the opponents of the Sunday Cinemas Bill would work wonders.

CHAPTER THREE

The Trespass

Sunday, April 24, dawned clear and bright. Early in the morning I was off to Hayfield with my friend and colleague, Woolfie Winnick. We went on our bikes as both of us were keen cyclists. This was fortunate because, as I was to learn later, the police had obtained an injunction to restrain me from going on the Trespass, and had spent a fruitless week trying to serve it on me. Apparently, whenever they called at my home I was out and nobody could inform them of my whereabouts. On the morning of April 24 they were on watch at London Road Station to serve the injunction on me. Fortunately for me and unfortunately for the police, I never went near the station. It is hard to speculate what would have happened if they had served me with the injunction.

En route to Hayfield, Woolfie and I discussed possible routes on to Kinder, and alternative venues for our meeting if Hayfield recreation ground should prove unsuitable. When we reached Hayfield we went to a tea-room, had a drink of tea and stored away our bikes and then went to survey the intended trespass. We spent about two and a half to three hours looking at possible routes. On the tops we could see clusters of gamekeepers lurking on the look-out,

and after finally deciding that William Clough - Sandy Heys - Kinder was our best bet, we returned to Hayfield. On our way back we passed a number of possible sites for our meeting. One was a flat space at the end of Kinder Road, and another a disused quarry close by. The quarry was the most convenient as a projecting rock formed a platform overlooking a natural amphitheatre below.

It must have been about one o'clock when we got back to Hayfield and the picture had

KEITH WARRENDER

completely changed. From a quiet, deserted village it had become a packed centre of activity. Police were everywhere. We learned later that one third of the Derbyshire police force, under the personal command of the Derbyshire Deputy Chief Constable, was concentrated in and around the village, and some were stationed in a local cinema.

Opposite page: William Clough
Above: Hayfield Church

The recreation ground was full of ramblers, and still more were coming from the tea-rooms and cafes. Woolfie and I melted into the crowd, to meet our mates. Again it was very fortunate for me. I learned later that the police had been on watch at Hayfield Station to serve me with their injunction, and were even on the look-out for me at the recreation ground.

We gathered a small group of our committee together. It was obvious that it would be very easy for the police to trap the crowd in the recreation ground. This was at a lower level than the surrounding roads and exits could easily be blocked. We did not know what the police intentions were, but we were not prepared to take any chances of the day's events finishing up at the recreation ground before the walk had even started, so we decided to move off before the appointed time of 2pm. We learned later in evidence given by council officials that meetings were not permitted in the recreation ground. We sent our colleagues through the crowd and into the adjoining cafes, telling ramblers to move quietly into Kinder Road.

Left: The protesters gather at Hayfield recreation ground.

Below: Scaling a wall at the recreation ground when the organisers realized the danger of being trapped by the police.

Soon a small army of ramblers was on the march, estimated by the Press at about 400. The police were caught on the hop. They could not get in front of the ramblers to stop us (short of fighting their way through our ranks), nor could they use their vehicles because of the nature of the road. As they could not predict which way we would turn when we reached the end of the road, it was impossible for them to head us off. So they fell in ignominiously behind the ramblers.

On we marched, cheerfully singing and talking, until we reached the first alternative meeting site. We stopped to hold our meeting but were immediately approached by Stockport Waterworks' officials who warned us that meetings on their property were prohibited. We did not want a battle with the Stockport water authority on this issue and so we moved off to the quarry site. This was by far the better site from every point of view, both acoustically and strategically. I scrambled onto the natural pulpit and started to address the crowd below.

It was an inspiring picture. There were hundreds of young men and women in their picturesque rambling gear: shorts of every length and colour, flannels and breeches, even overalls, vivid colours and drab khaki, (khaki shorts and shirts were fashionable at the time), multi-coloured sweaters and pullovers, army packs and rucksacks of every size and shape. (It was the 'done thing' at that time to carry enormous rucksacks crammed to capacity.)

Without any preliminaries I started to speak. Originally it had been intended that I would be chairman and that Jack, one of the older members, would address the meeting. He was a very good speaker with an excellent knowledge of the history of the fight for 'Access to Mountains', but unfortunately he felt unable to do this on the day. He got hold of me and said 'I don't think I'd better speak. It might have an effect on my job'. As there was not time to find a replacement I had to fill the gap. It did not really matter because I had a most sympathetic audience. They laughed at any semblance of a joke, and when I had finished they gave me a tremendous round of applause. I very briefly outlined the history of the injustice of enclosures, which had stolen common land from the people in

Chance meeting with one of the original water board officials, Horace Oldham, during the making of the BBC's reconstruction of the Trespass in the 1970 'Look Stranger' series. Oldham said to Rothman 'I never forget a face, Nussbaum isn't it?' Benny replied 'This is one face you have forgotten, it's Rothman'. Oldham had mixed him up with one of the other charged trespassers who was better known as Dave Nesbitt.

a fraudulent series of so-called Enclosure Acts. I sketched the history of the 'Access to Mountains' agitation from its inception in 1884, nearly 50 years earlier, and the ruthless landowners' lobby which had frustrated any effort to pass the Bill through Parliament. I called for the Mass Trespass as a start to a campaign to backup the other organisations fighting for 'Access to Mountains'.

Benny Rothman (left), in his cycling gear, addressing the crowd at Bowden Bridge quarry, with Lance Helman. Woolfie Winnick is circled (lower left of photo)

WILLOW PUBLISHING

I denied stories in the media that said we were hooligans intent on trouble. We were not intending to injure or damage anybody or anything. We wanted a peaceful demonstration ramble, but were determined not to be diverted or stopped. I gave instructions on the 'whistle signals' we would use to control the ramble -

one blast for stop, two for turn right, three for advance in open formation. Then amid tremendous applause from the walkers, I scrambled off the speaker's rock and into the crowd. As I did so, Woolfie blew the whistle for the start of the ramble and was leading the walkers along the road towards William Clough.

As I reached the crowd, a small group of BWSF ramblers surrounded me acting as an informal bodyguard. They were determined that there should be no arrests, and none was made as we started the second leg of our demonstration.

Along the road towards Kinder Reservoir we marched, cheerful and jubilant, with the police in the rear. At the meeting the police had adopted a low profile, keeping to the fringes of the crowd. Now they re-grouped at the rear of the ramblers. As we went through gates, over brooks and stiles, the front sections of the

KEITH WARRENDER

Opposite top: 'General Rothman', as one newspaper nicknamed him, re-visiting the quarry in 1982. Not everyone at the original meeting was in favour of the trespass and there were reports of heckling.

Opposite below: Among the ramblers can be seen trilby-hatted water board officials, police and reporters. The inset shows Edward Beever, the keeper who was injured in the protest.

Top: Following the meeting in the quarry, the crowd on their way towards William Clough.

Above: Left: Benny and his minder - Woolfie are circled.

ramblers waited until the whole group emerged, then carried on. This prevented any arrests along the route.

Up the steep bank on to White Brow we scrambled, admiring the Kinder Reservoir below, and then on to Nab Brow and the William Clough footpath. The whole body of ramblers was now well into William Clough. At the point agreed earlier between Woolfie and myself, roughly about one-third to a half of the distance to Ashop Head, Woolfie, who was leading the ramble, blew his whistle for a right turn. Our stewards in the body of the ramblers turned right, then the crowd of ramblers commenced a slow scramble up the face towards the top of Kinder Scout in a long 'open formation' line. This was to ensure that if any section was stopped, the rest would still be able to carry on and achieve the objective.

About half-way up the scramble groups of gamekeepers emerged shouting to the ramblers to stop, and threatening us with their sticks. There were probably only three or four groups of keepers along the whole line, about 20 to 30 men in all. One temporary keeper, Edward Beever, became involved in a scuffle in which he was hurt, though not seriously, as he was able to walk back to Hayfield. Most keepers brandished their sticks and threatened to use

Inset: The first view of the keepers as the protesters moved off the William Clough footpath, as recreated in the 'Look Stranger' programme. Above: The probable point where the ramblers left William Clough.

The keepers can be seen using their sticks. 'Woolfie' Winnick in the light top (centre)
was in the thick of the action with possibly the keeper, Beever, on the ground.

33

them if the ramblers did not turn back, but wisely did nothing but bluster as the ramblers pushed them aside and carried on.

One or two, however, did use their sticks on ramblers, and were promptly disarmed. Woolfie was struck on the head by a keeper. Unfortunately for the keeper, Woolfie was, among other things, a competent amateur boxer, and a very much wiser keeper nursed a painful jaw. As the long line of ramblers scrambled uphill, one group came upon a nest with a bird sitting on its eggs. They promptly put a picket on the nest to make sure that the bird was not disturbed. I encountered no keepers on my section of the front.

As we approached the top of the scramble another big group was seen on the skyline. For a moment or two we braced ourselves for a major encounter, and were very relieved when we were greeted by an enthusiastic group of supporters from Sheffield, who had come via Edale, and late-comers from the Manchester area who had come by other routes. We learned from them that every railway station en route was teeming with police and that there were police patrols on the roads. We exchanged congratulations and experiences, and decided to hold a victory meeting.

I addressed the crowd again, together with a Sheffield rambler. Jack Clayton of the Manchester BWSF committee also spoke. We were on the holy of holies, the forbidden territory of Kinder. So far there had been no arrests and no direct police

Above: The keepers confront the trespassers.

Left: Edward Beever, the injured keeper, receiving first aid.

Opposite top: The Kinder plateau from the top of William Clough where the trespassers congregated.

Opposite below: Looking down William Clough towards Hayfield - the return route of the protesters.

KEITH WARRENDER

interference, but we wondered whether this position would change. We decided to go back as we had come, one strong, united body, and not disperse in all directions like a band of criminals. It was by no means a schoolboy prank with everybody trying to pretend they had not been involved. It was a demonstration for the rights of ordinary people to walk on land stolen from them in earlier times; we were proud of our effort and proudly marched back the way we had come, the Manchester group to Hayfield and the Sheffield group to Edale.

Did the trespassers reach Kinder Scout?

The evidence suggests that after the confrontation with the keepers on Sandy Heys Moor, Benny and his associates made their way up to Ashop Head, below the Kinder plateau, where they stopped to hold their meeting. From there they looked up and saw the Sheffield contingent arriving. John Watson, the head keeper on the Kinder estate, watched the events unfold and has since confirmed the trespassers did not reach the plateau. However, by going off the legal William Clough path, the protesters had made their point. The day will always be known as the Kinder Trespass even though it happened on the moor below. Nevertheless two trespasses took place over Kinder that day, because the Sheffield contingent, who joined the protesters at Ashop Head, came from Edale station via Jacob's Ladder and later returned the same way. (KW)

The Trespassers

Mr Barnes, Stockport
Clem Beckett, Oldham
Ernest Beesley, Manchester
George & Florence Boatte
M Bobker, Whitefield
Noel Bradshaw, Salford
Bob Brown, Sheffield
Mrs H Brown, Urmston
Issey & Jackie Brown, Manchester
Mr Chapman
Mr & Mrs Clarke
Jack Clayton, Manchester
John Cleary, Sheffield
Jud Clyne, (Sydney)
Max Clyne, Manchester
J Cohen, Manchester
H Colley, Manchester
Bella Costello, Manchester
Lilian Crabtree
J Daintree, Altrincham
Dorothy Davies, (London)
Peter Davies, (London)
John Davies, (Essex)
L Dixon, (London)
Harold Doughty, New Mills
Mrs C Eccles, Lytham
Alan Edwards, Stockport
Helen Edwards, Stockport
Mrs Finley
Frank Fisher, Sheffield
N Frayman, Manchester
Sol Gadian, Manchester
Joseph Garnett, Stockport

Tona Gillett, (Surrey)
Harold Glencroft, Salford
Wilfred Green, (Spalding)
Walter Greenhalgh, (London)
Eli Hague, (Leicester)
Eric Hague
George Haigh, Stockport
Gordon Hallam, Hayfield
Jean Heath, (New Zealand)
Lance Helman, Cheadle
Charles Hinchcliffe, Sheffield
Emily Hodgkiss, Salford
Sol Holt, Manchester
David Hughes, Manchester
Abe Jacobs, Prestwich
E Jessop, Nottingham
Jimmy Jones, Manchester
Riv Keats, Manchester
Bill Keen, Sheffield
Mrs Lea, Stockport
George, Doris & Raymond Leather
Walter Leigh, Glossop
M Levine, Hale
Nell Logan, (Wiltshire)
Celia Lloyd, Manchester
I Luft, Manchester
Jack Mansfield, Glossop
Walter Martin
Harry Mendel, (Australia)
Charlotte Olive Merrington, Chinley
H Middleton, Wirral
Jimmy Miller, Salford
Harold Morris, Manchester
Joseph Norman

Dave Nussbaum, Manchester
Bill O'Donnel
Eric Oliver, Sheffield
Mrs D Parkinson, Stockport
Francis Edward Poole, Salford
P Poole, London
George Revill, Sheffield
Charles Richardson, Sheffield
Benny Rothman, Timperley
Harry Rowley, Manchester
Arthur Schofield, Stockport
Alice Shaw, Stockport
Albert Shirtcliffe, Doncaster
John Simmonds, Hayfield
Max & Margaret Slater, (Australia)
G Smith, Sheffield
Edith Stringer, Manchester
George Sumner, Blackpool
Tom Sutton, Manchester
AJP Taylor
Sir Michael Tippett, London
Victor Wall, (Cambridge)
GH Webster, Morecambe
Elizabeth Wilde, Salford
Frank and Doris Wilson, Sheffield
Woolfie Winnick, Manchester
M Wiseberg, Manchester
Gordon Womersley, Sheffield
Len Wood
Harry Woolfenden, Sheffield
Harry Wyatt, Manchester

Many of the names are from a participators' list made by Benny Rothman at the time of the 1982 Trespass Anniversary celebration. It does not necessarily mean that they were all alive at this time, and some may have just been guests at the celebration. The locations were those currently known.

The list was not comprehensive and other known participants have been added. There were many more on the Trespass and the publisher would like to know the names of others who took part, for the purposes of further research.

WILFRED GREEN a keen rambler from Pontefract had trespassed regularly on Kinder and the surrounding moors prior to the protest. For a day out on the hills he had to catch the first bus to Leeds and then a tram out towards Derbyshire. He often came across keepers barring his way and remembered having many heated arguments. The challenge of evading keepers and farmers was all part of the fun for him. He said it was common knowledge among ramblers that the Mass Trespass was going to happen. Handbills about the planned protest had been passed round the regular Sunday ramblers. He recalled walking on the day with a small group but was not involved in any scuffles nor did he see any arrests.

ERNEST BEESLEY like many others had been frustrated by the lack of progress in getting access to Kinder Scout. He realised that taking part in the Trespass was an illegal act, but hoped it might bring change where peaceful methods had failed. Ernest recalled that after the Trespass they walked back into Hayfield singing 'It's a long way to Tipperary' and other songs. In later years he campaigned with CND and helped set up a branch in Levenshulme.

George and Doris Leather

RAYMOND LEATHER from Eccles was just three when he was taken on the Trespass by his parents, George and Doris. He doesn't remember the day, but was told that his father got a black eye during the struggle with the keepers. Probably Raymond was being looked after by his mother in William Clough when the trouble started. He thought there were other families on the protest. He and his parents used to go to the camps at a farm in Rowarth, and later he organised hiking and cycling weekends for Eccles YHA.

NOEL BRADSHAW and **ELIZABETH WILDE** from Broughton, who later married, were on the Trespass with a group of ramblers. Their group branched off before the confrontation with the keepers and made their way to the top of the hill where they joined the main group. Later on, as they travelled back, the police were on the train questioning people about the Trespass.

PEAK DISTRICT NATIONAL PARK AUTHORITY

L-R: Harvey Jackson, George Sumner, Benny Rothman, Peter Jackson and Walter Leigh at the 1992 reunion

A policeman's tale

In 1932 1 was an 18 year-old apprentice living on Mottram Road, Stalybridge. In those days we worked from Monday to Saturday with only Sunday off. This was the day we loved to head for the Derbyshire hills with friends.

We knew the moors were closed to public access but could not see why we should not be allowed to walk on them. We did no harm as we all loved and respected wildlife and the countryside. Many times we had confrontations with landowners, keepers and agents.

Our usual route was from Stalybridge through Mottram, Charlesworth, Monks Road to the top of Chunal and onto the moorland to Mill Hill with Kinder Downfall as our destination. We had heard about the planned trespass and protest and decided to do our usual walk and hopefully meet up with the main party which we did near the top of Kinder. When the party started to move back down to Hayfield we joined them and on arriving in the village found a large party of police and landowners and staff.

The officer in charge of the police was Assistant Chief Constable James Main Garrow, who I was to meet up with in years to come. Leaders of the party were soon picked out and arrested. Getting arrested and taken to court could lead you to losing your job

so we decided to avoid trouble by retracing our steps to the top of Chunal and head home. On arriving there we were met by a group of so-called keepers, more like hired thugs, who set about us with sticks and boots, gave us a savage beating then pushed us into a bed of nettles. We did not dare complain as this would have been trouble for us.

We later read about the court proceeding and imprisonment of Benny Rothman and the others and the prejudiced way they were prosecuted. In 1935 1 applied to join the police service and went to Derby for interview. I had a large head of bright ginger hair and was always known as 'Ginger Jackson'. The interview panel was chaired by none other than the now Chief Constable Garrow. He gave me a hard stare as if he thought he had seen me before. Looking at my application he saw my pastimes were swimming and hill walking. He said to me quite firmly 'Jackson we do not like hill walkers in Derbyshire, they are not welcome'.

This did not put me off. I served my time in the force, my son Peter followed me into the Derbyshire police and adopted my love of the hills. He served in the Peak District nearly all his service, and spent many years in the Mountain Rescue Service and as a part-time National Park Ranger.

HARVEY JACKSON

The Trespassers

ALAN EDWARDS was aged two at the time of the Kinder Mass Trespass. He was taken along by his elder sister and a friend. Their boyfriends came along just to keep an eye on them. Alan was told that the girls were not allowed to be in the area where the confrontation with the keepers took place. Afterwards, according to his family, all Alan could remember of the occasion was being surrounded by 'lots of bare legs'.

Frank Wilson

Arthur Schofield

John Simmonds

Bill Keen

George Sumner

Nell Logan

WALTER LEIGH had been chased off the Kinder and Bleaklow moors on several occasions by keepers with large sticks. He used to cycle from his home in Dukinfield and hide his bike in a hedgerow before setting off on a walk.

On the day of the Trespass, nine weeks before his nineteenth birthday, he was descending William Clough and saw a crowd of people. He asked what it was all about and was informed it was a Mass Trespass for freedom to walk the hills. He was invited to join in and did so willingly, as walking the hills was a great joy to him. After walking some distance, he remembered seeing a gamekeeper lashing out with his stick at the walkers who cheered and jeered. The remainder of the walk went peacefully for him and he continued to enjoy the peace and wonder of the hills for the rest of his life.

GARY LEIGH

Kinder Scout with Kinder Reservoir (left) and William Clough above the reservoir

Manchester Evening Chronicle

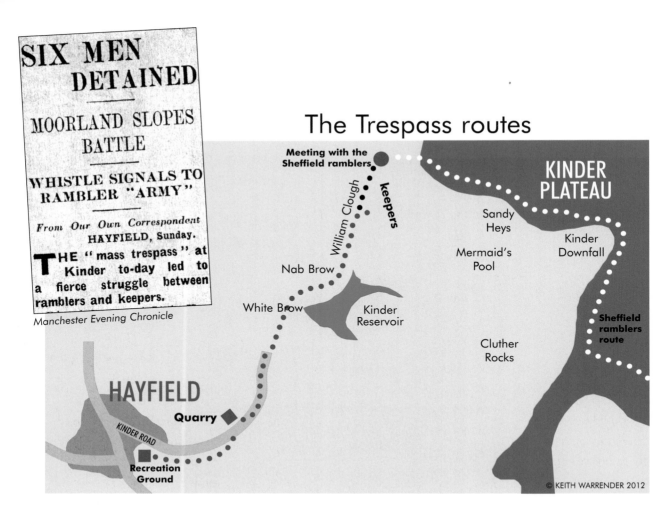

The Trespass routes

Meeting with the Sheffield ramblers

KINDER PLATEAU

keepers

William Clough

Sandy Heys

Mermaid's Pool

Kinder Downfall

Nab Brow

White Brow

Kinder Reservoir

Cluther Rocks

Sheffield ramblers route

HAYFIELD

Quarry

KINDER ROAD

Recreation Ground

© KEITH WARRENDER 2012

The former lock-up at Hayfield which had been proposed as a Kinder Trespass exhibition centre

KEITH WARRENDER

42

Arrest and Trial

The police who had not faced the scramble uphill on to Kinder, had returned to Hayfield for further re-grouping and fresh orders. They were instructed to make some arrests; consequently when we returned to Hayfield we were faced with a strong force of police stretched across Kinder Road, which brought us to a halt.

Hayfield lock-up

We stopped the ramblers and waited. It would have been counter-productive to try to break through and start a battle with the police. We had achieved our objective, the next move was with the establishment.

Some policemen, accompanied by keepers, moved across the ranks of the ramblers and made five arrests. There was no attempt on our part to resist, nor was there any effort made to rescue any of those arrested. I was among those taken to Hayfield lock-up for interrogation and to be charged.

When we arrived at the lock-up we found that another rambler had previously been arrested at the scene of the scuffle with the injured special keeper. He, it seems, was one of the few ramblers opposed to the Mass Trespass. He had gone along, following in the rear of the ramblers. On seeing the scuffle and the keeper on the ground he claims he went forward to assist him. He was an easy target, so the police promptly arrested him and took him back to Hayfield at the time when the main body of ramblers was either still scrambling on to Kinder Scout, or on Kinder at the meeting with our Sheffield group.

Inside the lock-up we had our names taken. There was great excitement among the police when I gave my name, as they had been on the look-out for me all day to serve me with the injunction. I do not know what description of me had been given, or how they had proposed to identify me. In evidence at the various court hearings, at New Mills and at Derby, the police witnesses claimed to have arrested me because they recognised me as the speaker at the quarry, but they certainly did not know that the speaker was the man for whom they had been searching during the preceding week. The ramblers arrested were John Anderson, aged 21, arrested at the scene of the scuffle with a temporary keeper; Jud Clynes, aged 23; Harry Mendel, aged 23; David Nussbaum, aged 19; Arthur (Tona) Gillett, aged 19; and myself, Bernard Rothman, aged 20.

Meanwhile outside, a big body of ramblers waited for us to be released. When about an

New Mills Police station today. The building is now a private property with a plaque unveiled by Benny Rothman in 1994 commemorating the Trespass.

KEITH WARRENDER

hour or so had elapsed and we were still being kept in custody, the elected spokesmen hammered on the door, offered bail on our behalf, and pressed for our release.

The situation was beginning to look ugly, so the police smuggled us out through a rear door and took us to New Mills police station.

We were kept overnight at New Mills. With hindsight, I now realise that we should have challenged this at the time. The year was 1932, the telephone had been invented, and the excuse of establishing our identities before we could be released, was very thin indeed. Verification could have been made in an hour or two at the most.

The real reason was, of course, that the establishment had been very badly hurt by the event, and could not decide with what we were to be charged. The next day, when we appeared at New Mills police court we were all charged with unlawful assembly and breach of the peace, and were remanded on bail until 11 May. John

Anderson was also charged with causing grievous bodily harm to Edward Beever, a temporary keeper, and similarly remanded on that charge.

We duly appeared at the New Mills court on 11th May. On the first day of the case the charges were read out. John Anderson's case was to be considered at a special hearing later.

It is significant that no charges of trespass or damage were brought against anybody, in spite of the fact that this was the reason for all the events. We were all first offenders; none of us had ever before been in a court. Arthur (Tona) Gillett, who came from a wealthy banking family, was represented in court, as were John Anderson, Jud Clynes, Dave Nussbaum and Harry Mendel; I conducted my own defence.

This had been decided upon by the BWSF Committee as it was thought that no solicitor was likely to conduct the defence on the basis of history and politics. We were later criticised by some leaders of the rambling movement for not engaging an outstanding barrister, but at the time they neither offered us any help, nor suggested that we do this.

The police brought a considerable number of detectives of all ranks and police constables as witnesses, in addition to keepers, and employees of Hayfield Council and Stockport Waterworks. Not a single private citizen from the district was produced by the prosecution to justify their claim that the proposed Mass Trespass had caused fear or apprehension in the minds of people in the district. The Court then adjourned and resumed the next day. On this occasion, only Gillett was legally represented. The defence brought no witnesses. The cost of travel and the loss of wages it would have involved, deterred any witnesses from testifying on our behalf.

SEQUEL TO HIKERS' PROTEST

CHARGES FOLLOW ALLEGED TRESPASS

LORD BIG BUG

NOTICES POSTED ON A DOOR

From Our Special Correspondent

NEW MILLS, Wednesday.

SIX young men were accused at the police court here to-day with offences alleged to have been committed during the mass trespass on Kinder Scout on April 24.

EVENING CHRONICLE

LARGEST EVENING SALE IN THE PROVINCES.

No. 10,856.   (Registered as a Newspaper.)   MONDAY, APRIL 25, 1932.   ONE PENNY.

10 LAST EDITION

Beatty Bros Cheviot & Saxon Sports Suits 62'- MANCHESTER, Oldham, Bolton, Blackburn, Rochdale, Leigh, Northwich, Henley, Hyde

KINDER SCOUT RAMBLERS IN COURT.

STORY OF HAND-TO-HAND FIGHT.

INJURED KEEPER IN HOSPITAL AFTER MASS TRESPASS.

CLASH WHEN CROWD SURGED OVER HILLSIDE.

FROM OUR OWN CORRESPONDENT.
NEW MILLS, MONDAY.

SIX ramblers appeared at New Mills Police Court to-day on charges arising out of the "mass trespass" on Kinder Scout yesterday afternoon.

John Thomas Anderson (21), cotton piecer, of The Quadrant, Cemetery-road, Droylsden, was remanded to a special court on May 11 on a charge of doing grievous bodily harm to Edward Beever, a special keeper, at Hayfield yesterday.

Anderson was further charged with Julius Clyne (23),

City Unemployed Demonstration.

Manchester and Salford unemployed to-day took part in a mass demonstration to urge the commencing of big relief schemes. The pictures show a view of part of the procession, and a group of women demonstrators.

MASS MARCH OF UNEMPLOYED.

ARMED MADMAN SCARES WOMAN.

FACING PISTOL ALONE IN TRAIN.

REFLECTION IN WINDOW.

An alarming experience which befell a Manchester woman when confronted by a lunatic with a loaded revolver in a train travelling between Romiley and Manchester, was told to the EVENING CHRONICLE to-day.

Mrs. Fred Mather, of Tavistock-street, Harpurhey, was returning from a visit to relatives at Romiley and was alone in the compartment when a man, who only a short time previously had been certified as insane, got in and pointed a revolver at her.

Mrs. Mather pulled the communication cord, but as the man continued to act strangely she then opened the door and stepped on to the footboard. Swinging his legs outside, the carriage the man started to follow her.

THE PREMIER'S EYES.

TWO CHILDREN BURNED TO DEATH

TRAPPED IN HOUSE FIRE WHILE ASLEEP.

REFUSAL TO LEAVE FROM WINDOW.

Two little girls were burned to death and their infant brother seriously injured as the result of a fire which occurred to-day at their home in Hythe-street, Halton, Leeds.

The dead children are: Nellie Connell, aged 11, and Margaret Connell, aged eight.

The fire broke out while they were asleep above the shop occupied by their father, Mr. Joseph Connell.

FIREMEN'S DISCOVERY.

The fire was discovered by the wife of a neighbouring doctor who gave the alarm and tried to persuade the children to jump from the window.

After subduing the flames the firemen found the children in the bedroom above the shop fatally burned.

They were taken to Leeds Infirmary, where their brother, Alfred, aged five, lies in a serious condition.

WILLOW PUBLISHING

KINDER SCOUT RAMBLERS

The prosecution witnesses were questioned by the defence solicitors and by myself, and finally I made a defence submission which was carefully taken down in longhand by the Clerk of the Court. He was outraged at the length of the statement, and constantly interrupted me, but I carried on until I had finished what I had to say. This took about seventy-five minutes, to the great indignation of the prosecution.

My statement dealt with the unhappy state of affairs in towns and cities for young people, and their desire for the open country; the over-crowding and unsatisfactory state of footpaths at peak periods at weekends and holiday times; and the injustice of the filching of the Derbyshire moorlands for grouse shooting. It put forward the belief of the BWSF. in the need for mass action by ramblers if access to mountains was to be achieved. It pointed to examples of successes achieved in the past by ramblers in saving foot-paths. It then analysed the prosecution evidence, pointing to contradictory statements made by police and other witnesses. It finally dealt with the scuffles which ensued, and refuted any suggestion of hooliganism or incited violence

Three of the accused from the 'Look Stranger' programme - L to R Benny Rothman, Dave Nesbitt and Tona Gillett.

RIOT CHARGES

On 'Change To-da

on the part of the ramblers, pointing out that the only violence which occurred came from stick-wielding keepers.

The submission concluded: 'The demonstration of 24 April was a peaceful demonstration to gain support for our contention of the right of access to mountains. The assembly at the quarry, if that is the assembly which is alleged to be an unlawful assembly, gave no-one any reason to fear a breach of the peace. If this is correct I simply plead not guilty to the charge'. All my colleagues also pleaded not guilty. The court decided to commit all the ramblers to the Derby Assizes which opened on 29 June.

The special hearing against John Anderson took place a week later at New Mills and he was remanded to Derby Assizes on the charge of causing grievous bodily harm to special keeper Edward Beever, in addition to the other charges made against the rest of us. When Anderson appeared he was not represented by a solicitor, nor were any witnesses on his behalf present in Court. The witnesses for the prosecution were a detective inspector, two detective sergeants and a detective constable. In addition the clerk of the court, according to newspaper reports at the time, was very belligerent, hectoring Anderson and contradicting him. Anderson pleaded not guilty, and was remanded to the assizes.

Previous protests

Although the Kinder Trespass was to become perhaps the best-known demonstration against access restrictions it was not the first. In September 1847 a party of naturalists led by a university professor was stopped from using a road at Glen Tilt in the Highlands. The highway had been in public use for many years before the land-owner, the Duke of Atholl, put up gates.

● Two thousand people came out to protest in October 1887 against the threatened closure of a public right of way between Keswick and Latrigg Hill.

● Colonel Ainsworth, owner of land around Winter Hill, blocked off a previously used road in 1896 which prompted up to ten thousand protesters to walk along it. A demonstration the following week attracted a crowd of around two thousand.

● Miss Benett of Burslem was brought to court in March 1905 for leading a group over a route on the Duke of Sutherland's Trentham estate which had been in public use for at least ninety years.

● The Sheffield Clarion Ramblers Club along with other organisations regularly walked the disputed Roman Doctor's Gate route between 1909 and 1927 until it was authorised as a legal byway.

● Nearly two thousand attended a protest over the closure of the ancient Benfield footpath near Werneth Low in March 1927.

● Over six hundred took part in a trespass over the obstruction of a footpath previously used by the public at Dutton near Blackburn in October 1930. (KW)

PEAK ASSAULTS CHARGES

Trial Resumed of Six Manchester Youths

From Our Own Correspondent

DERBY, Thursday.

Whether the crowd were trespassing or not was immaterial, but it might be material that the crowd were told they were trespassing.

This was the remark made by Mr. Justice Acton at Derby Assizes to-day when the hearing was resumed of the case in which six Manchester youths are charged with riotous assembly and assault at Hayfield, in the Peak district.

The defendants are:—

John Thomas Anderson (21), cotton piercer, The Quadant, Cemetery Road, Droylsden; Bernard Rothman, store-keeper, Granton-street, Cheetham; Julius Clyne (23), machinist, Elizabeth-street, Cheetham; Harry Mendel (22), machinist, Townley-street, Cheetham; Anthony Walter Gillett (19), student, Banboo' Road, Oxfor, care of the Dalton Hall, Manchester University; and David Nussbaum (19), labourer, Red Bank, Cheetham.

Further Charges

Rothman, Clyne, and Mussbaum were also charged with incitement, and there was a further charge against Anderson of inflicting grievous bodily harm on Edward Beever, the keeper of the Stockport Corporation waterworks at Hayfield.

The affair occurred on April 24, when a demonstration was arranged by the British Workers' Sports Federation to obtain the right of access to the Kinder Scout.

Manchester Evening Chronicle

CHAPTER FIVE

Derby Assizes

The next stage was at the Derby Assizes and took place on 21 and 22 July - sixty miles from the homes of the ramblers. This made it impossible for the Defence to muster any witnesses, as the cost would now be very much higher, and would also have to include possible overnight hotel expenses. On this occasion only Gillett and Anderson were legally represented, the remainder of the ramblers not being too happy at the manner in which legal representatives had acted in the lower courts.

Ted Rivers, who had researched the trial in the journal The Progressive Rambler for April 1942 wrote, 'The most remarkable feature of the trial was the composition of the grand jury ('grand' is certainly the word). Here were six ramblers charged with offences connected with walking on a piece of land which in the past had been stolen from the people by grasping landowners. Of what did this grand jury - that central feature of British justice - consist? Local grocers and candlestick makers perhaps? Certainly not. These ramblers were tried before a jury consisting of two brigadier-generals, three colonels, two majors, three captains and two aldermen..'

We also found that the charges had been altered. Previously the main charge had been that of 'unlawful assembly'. We now found that the charge stated 'They riotously assembled

Beever the keeper can just be seen on the ground amongst the crowd.

together, and that they riotously assembled together and assaulted Edward Beever'. In addition I was charged with inciting various persons to riot and assault. Anderson was additionally charged with occasioning actual bodily harm.

Comment on the trial in the Progressive Rambler magazine April 1940

The whole apparatus of the state was now brought to bear to intimidate the ramblers. The pomp and ceremony of the bewigged judges and barristers in their medieval robes, the atmosphere in court with police, ushers, and now with prison warders in attendance, all cast a threatening atmosphere over the proceedings.

Even before the hearing I had been receiving some private intimidation. In the week prior to the hearing my home had been visited by 'officials' who claimed that they were from Strangeways prison. They wanted to know how often I went out during the week, who my companions were, and all about me. Unfortunately, I was not present when these alleged 'officials' arrived, or I should have tried to find out who they really were and the purpose of their enquiries. They didn't frighten me, but they certainly frightened my mother and sisters.

49

Edward Beever, the injured keeper, was taken to hospital in Stockport and discharged later. However he was sent back the next day and stayed in hospital for a week. He had stomach injuries and a sprained ankle.
Sadly, he died five years later from an infection, after cutting himself while chopping wood at home.
He joined the Regular Army before the first World War and was later wounded in France. At the time of the Trespass he was employed by Stockport Waterworks department at Kinder.

ABSTRACT OF INDICTMENT

<pre>
                THE KING   v.   BERNARD ROTHMAN

                               DAVID NUSSBAUM

                               JOHN THOMAS ANDERSON

                               JULIUS CLYNE

                               ANTHONY WALTER GILLETT, and

                               HARRY MENDEL.
</pre>

(Mendel was found not guilty on all charges and dismissed.)

DERBYSHIRE SUMMER ASSIZES 1932

HOLDEN AT DERBY

THE INDICTMENT CHARGES BERNARD ROTHMAN, DAVID NUSSBAUM, JOHN THOMAS ANDERSON, JULIUS CLYNE, ANTHONY WALTER GILLETT, and HARRY MENDEL WITH THE FOLLOWING OFFENCES.

FIRST COUNT

Statement of offence.
Riot and Assault.

Particulars of Offence.

BERNARD ROTHMAN, DAVID NUSSBAUM, JOHN THOMAS ANDERSON, JULIUS CLYNE, ANTHONY WALTER GILLETT and HARRY MENDEL and other persons unknown, on the 24th day of April 1932 in the County of Derby riotously assembled together and assaulted Edward Beever.

ALL NOT GUILTY.

A copy of the Indictment at Derby Assizes

Another little incident in the early part of the trial shows the malice of the judge, Sir Edward Acton, and the cavalier manner in which he tried to squash and belittle us. Owing to the fact that we were strangers in Derby and had difficulty in finding a reasonable cafe near the Court for a drink and sandwich during the dinner interval, five of us were 10 minutes late in arriving back. (Tona Gillett was having lunch with his father at a hotel). Judge Acton could not have been more vicious. He did not give us the opportunity to explain, or apologise. He put on an act of outraged indignation and stormed and raged about 'contempt of court'. He told us that for this 'contempt' we would be kept in custody overnight, a further intimidation. It gave us a taste of things to come, a night in the cells at Leicester jail with all the bombast and bullying

of prison discipline, with no opportunity for a discussion of the day's and next day's proceedings between the men on trial.

I was not even allowed a light in my cell so that I could write up comments on the evidence which had been presented for my final defence submission. Still, it solved the problem for us of where to stay overnight without further expense.

The following day the prosecution team of police and keepers, well briefed and rehearsed, were called and made their statements. Minor items of interest were squeezed out of the witnesses in cross-examination. A detective inspector dealt with the events before the Trespass. His main purpose was to show the fear and apprehension in Hayfield caused by the proposed Trespass,

50

in order to establish the element in the charge that alarm was actually caused by the Trespass. He stated that he had received complaints in writing about the proposed Trespass, but would not reveal who the people were who complained, then made a monumental blunder by stating they were mainly 'people who own the land'.

That statement was the heart of the prosecution's case. It was the landowners who were afraid of the consequences of the Mass Trespass, and of the philosophy of mass action. Hence the trial. We had to be squashed, ramblers had to be taught a lesson, that behaviour of this kind would not be tolerated by the establishment.

Among other charges against me was one of inciting various persons to riot and assault. The main prosecution witness for this charge was a detective sergeant. He had been present at the meeting in the quarry and quoted in great detail statements which he alleged I had made, but he had written nothing down at the time, and was quoting from memory. Alas for him, he could not remember the words I actually used to 'incite the crowd to violence'. With more pressure from me he admitted that I had called for a disciplined, quiet and orderly demonstration, with no incitement to violence.

Judge Acton did cause some merriment in Court and at the same time instill prejudice into the case. A 'damning' piece of evidence had been presented. Tona Gillett was found to have in his possession, when arrested, a book by Lenin. To great laughter his lordship asked, 'Isn't that the Russian gentleman?'.

Then came my defence. I made a nine-page statement giving the history of the struggle for access to mountains and the policy of the BWSF and finally dealt with the Trespass itself. On the battle with the keepers I commented that 'there is only evidence from one witness of a blow being struck, and that is from a keeper who alleges he was struck with a buckle of a belt'.

I pointed to the contradictory evidence of all the witnesses to the scuffle where Beever sprained his ankle and received a stomach injury, with the number of ramblers ranging from a 'howling mob of 100 to 150', '12 to 20'

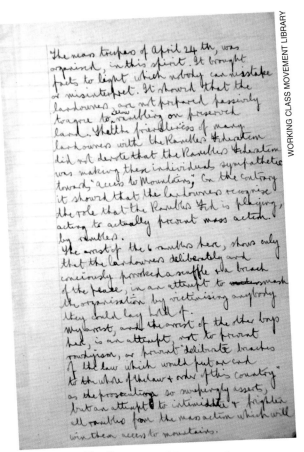

The first page of Benny Rothman's defence statement notes made in prison

At the time of the Trespass, Tona Gillett was 19 and preparing for entry to Cambridge via Manchester University. He was 6' 4" and during the scuffles he may have restrained a keeper who was wildly swinging a pickaxe handle. He came from a family of Quaker beliefs and at the trial was insultingly asked by the prosecuting counsel 'Did you quake on this occasion?'

As he and the others were waiting to be taken to prison, his mother, a member of the Clark's Shoes family, told him how proud she was of him. Gillett spent the time in prison preparing to read engineering at Cambridge. (See page 54 for his account of the Trespass).

He became deputy superintendent of Kingston power station in Surrey before founding a company in 1960 which made advanced microscopes. Later he moved into gas heating equipment manufacture.

Gillett was married twice and had ten grand-children. He died in 1992 age 80 following Parkinson's disease and heart problems. (KW)

and a statement concerning a 'general attack on Beever, dragging him downhill', with no witnesses actually having seen a single blow struck.

I commented that it seemed obvious that Beever started a scuffle with one rambler and a crowd of ramblers gathered around watching. I pointed out that the ramblers had no hesitation in return-ing to Hayfield. I asked, 'Would a gang of hooli-gans who had just indulged in a general riot, have returned to a small village which they knew was packed with police?' Nussbaum, Anderson, Gillett, Clyne and Mendel all pleaded not guilty.

The Judge took two hours in summing up, first directing that Mendel should be discharged through lack of evidence. Acton then said that no other country had such freedom of procession and demonstration as ours, and nobody would wish to see a curtailment of these rights. But the object of the prosecution was to prevent such things being done in a manner that amounted to a riot or unlawful assembly, and to strike terror in people's breasts.

Justice for all?

Compare the jail sentences of the Kinder Scout protesters to members of the Cheshire Hunt who were also accused of trespass. The hunters went onto land at Nantwich and got into an argument with the owner, a farmer. In attempting to resist the riders, the farmer was whipped nine times and received a head wound that needed stitches. The assailants were brought to police court at Broxton, but the charges were surprisingly dropped. It was later revealed that several members of the Bench were either members of, or associated with, the Cheshire Hunt. Despite being allegedly guilty of trespass and assault, the hunters escaped punishment - unlike their rambler counterparts from Manchester!

As reported in the Manchester Evening News, January 1933. (KW)

The acquitted trespasser

Harry Mendel was acquitted at the trial on a technicality. He was one of the organisers of the protest and a close friend of Benny Rothman. He deliberately kept out of the way of the photographers at Hayfield and the quarry to avoid detection. The severe response of the authorities to the Trespass shocked him and after that he was careful not to come into conflict with the law. He remembered being handcuffed at the trial at Derby after returning a few minutes late from lunch.

Born of Russian immigrants in Reddish, Harry was later very active in labour and union matters. He was a natural leader and organiser - from dances and sports to sing-songs. Later he became a factory manager but was sacked because he objected to the conditions imposed on the workers by new owners. Grateful factory staff organised a leaving party for him in recognition of his efforts.

Though physically small he was proud of his fitness. He took part in cycling races and liked to swim outdoors in winter.

During war service at El Alamein, Harry was hit by shrapnel which caused recurring health problems. He emigrated to New Zealand in the 1960s, and then at the age of eighty, he and his wife moved to Australia. He remained active and popular and there was a huge turnout at his funeral.

Another of the Trespass organisers, Woolfie Winnick, was a friend of Harry and his family. Woolfie became wealthy through a scrap metal business. His brother, Maurice, was a dance band leader and later promoted shows such as 'What's My Line' and 'Twenty Questions' to the BBC.   (KW)

The jury was absent for three quarters of an hour. Anderson was found not guilty of causing grievous bodily harm but guilty of assaulting Beever. I was found guilty of riotous assembly, together with the rest of the boys, and guilty of incitement to riotous assembly, but I was found not guilty of incitement of various persons to riot and assault. The sentences ranged from six months for Anderson, four months for me, two months each for Gillett and Clyne, three months for Nussbaum - one month more than Gillett' because he was found guilty of the very serious crime of selling the Daily Worker! Mendel was discharged.

Before sentencing Gillett, Judge Acton mildly reprimanded Tona for having become involved in 'such an unsavoury event'. Then came the question, 'aren't you ashamed of what you did?' It was obvious to me that Tona had merely to offer some form of apology in order to receive a reprimand and to be dismissed with a warning about his future conduct. That was something Tona was not prepared to do. He drew himself up to his full height, and looked the Judge full in the face. 'No sir, I would do it again' he answered.

We were then taken down to the cells of the Assize courts, and later transported by Black Maria to Leicester Jail. On the first day there we outraged the warders by trotting and jogging in the exercise yard. The authorities decided to split us up - Nesbitt went to Pentonville and Anderson to Wakefield. That seemed to be the end of the Mass Trespass. Or was it?

Why I went to jail
By Tona Gillett

About 500 people, mostly dressed in shorts, started from the Recreation ground. At a quarry we stopped and the secretary of the B.W.S.F. spoke to us. He ... emphasised that the use of force must be avoided if possible. None of us had any weapons and though we expected to meet with a few keepers, we imagined that the numbers would be too great for them and that they would be wise enough to let us alone.

On leaving the path we did meet eight keepers, armed with sticks. Owing to insufficient organisation, we made a tactical mistake. Instead of ignoring them, by walking round them, as we could very well have done, some of our people tried to go straight past them. In doing this the keepers naturally put up an opposition, and while a stick was being taken off one of them, he either fell and hurt himself in falling, or the knee of the fellow who was taking the stick from him, accidentally caught him in the stomach. The rights and wrongs of such an accident can never be settled. Each side has its own account.

In some circumstances it is necessary to use force, but here it was not. We did not intend to, and the fact that the stick was being taken from one of them, meant that he was too wild with it. However, everything was over in one or two minutes, and we went on until we joined the path again higher up. I saw one boy being walked off (by keepers as I thought), but I could not imagine that he could have been such a fool, as to have put himself in the hands of the keepers; so concluded it must be a hoax.

We marched back into Hayfield singing revolutionary songs and were then much astonished when five of us were arrested. I could not imagine what excuse they could find to arrest us for, but later, when inside the police station, we found that the boy, whom I had seen, was accused of hurting the keeper (presumably because he was the easiest to catch). We then realised that we might be in for anything.

The trial dragged on for two months and they eventually managed to convict us - not of trespass as might have been expected - but of riot. The poor fellow who was accused of doing 'Grievous Bodily Harm' to the keeper was given six months, and the secretary four months for 'Inciting'; two of us were given two months and one got off.

The rights of private property had been challenged. This is not a political offence, but a criminal offence. Thus 'British Justice' can convict and yet remain unpolitical. Needless to say, the punishment could have little effect on people with no sense of guilt; all their efforts to make us feel ashamed of ourselves increased our self-respect. The only positive results for us personally, is to leave us with a bitter hatred for those who have the power to do such things; and to confirm the opinions we already held.

The Trespass was certainly a success. It clearly frightened the authorities. It disillusioned at least the 500 present about British justice. Private Property had had to resort to force immediately its right to existence was challenged. About thirty extra police were called up; as many extra gamekeepers specially engaged; and I was told the reserves were out to prevent us from returning by another route.

GILLETT FAMILY

Tona receiving his MA in Engineering at Cambridge in 1936

Extract from an article in the university magazine 'Vanguard', November 1932, when Tona Gillett was a student at Manchester University

CHAPTER SIX

Not in Vain

The immediate reaction from the rambling public, from lovers of the open air, and from the public at large, was a greater awareness of the injustice of the situation and the need for access to mountains. Frank Turton, a prominent Sheffield figure in the open air movement, stated 'Thousands of ramblers went to view the scene of the Mass Trespass. National interest was aroused as never before.' The annual demonstration of ramblers at Winnats Pass, Castleton, on 26 June 1932 (that was even before the Derby assizes were held, and the sentences passed) brought an attendance of 10,000 ramblers - the biggest number in its history. A further mass trespass was held in Derbyshire at Abbey Brook in the Derwent Valley. Another, along Stanage Edge on 16 October, was stopped by mounted police and foot patrols with Alsatian dogs (unprecedented at the time).

A protest rally was held at Jacob's Ladder, at which Jud Clyne, among others, spoke. In the South a thousand-strong demonstration in support of access was held at Leith Hill, Surrey. Later, rallies for access were held both in Scotland and Wales.

In spite of their opposition to the Mass Trespass, the Manchester Ramblers' Federation officials, 'after careful consideration of all the circumstances', wrote to the Home Secretary appealing for the exercise of clemency' not only as an act of grace, but on the grounds of public policy'. Many other ramblers' federations in the country followed the example of the Manchester Federation and protested. The Home Secretary answered that he could find no grounds for any remission of sentences.

A flame had been lit and things could never be quite the same again. Time after time

The Jacob's Ladder rally in August 1932 in which Jud Clyne spoke of his increased determination to achieve more rights for ramblers.

WILLOW PUBLISHING

in negotiations with landowners they were reminded of the Mass Trespass when they were trying to kill negotiation by procrastination.

It is interesting to note that 56 per cent of all moorland and mountains to which the public now have access under the National Parks and Access to the Countryside Act of 1949, is in the Peak District. The first and largest National Park in Britain was the Peak District National Park. This was no accident. The history of struggle for access, the years of battles with gamekeepers and landowners, culminating in the Mass Trespass onto Kinder and the ensuing trespasses in

Winnats rally c1928

Derbyshire, left their mark on the landowners and legislators. It made the position of the ramblers' negotiators much stronger. The Mass Trespass was not in vain.

It is easy now to look back and see the mistakes made by the Mass Trespass organisers. We should never have antagonised the leadership of the Ramblers' Federation and those rambling leaders who had worked hard over a long period of time. We should perhaps have used our youthful zeal and energy inside the rambling movement, but of course, the faults were not all on one side.

Access to mountains as envisaged by the pioneers has still not been achieved. There are still vast tracts of mountain and moorland in Britain not covered by access agreements. New problems like the ploughing-up of moorland, exploration for minerals, and proposed reopening of long-disused mines in beauty spots and green belts arise from time to time.

Even today, plans for access can still be rejected. In this continuing effort to achieve unrestricted freedom to explore areas of outstanding natural beauty the lessons of the Mass Trespass over Kinder must never be forgotten.

Further protests

In the aftermath of the Kinder Trespass, there was a further protest at Abbey Brook near Sheffield in September 1932. It was organised by the Sheffield branch of the Ramblers' Rights Movement with around 200 people taking part. This time around one hundred keepers armed with pit props, assisted by the police, were able to drive back the ramblers off the moor. There had been a minor scuffle but no-one was arrested.

The following month the group organised a meeting at Burbage Bridge near Grindleford which was broken up by the police. The 200 ramblers reassembled on the moors near Longshaw where they heard speeches promoting the right of people to walk over land taken over by the Enclosure Acts.   (KW)

A record crowd attended the annual Winnats rally, following the Kinder Trespass. The speakers were occasionally heckled by the supporters of 'direct action' who later held their own rally. In the above photograph, Arthur Greenwood MP is addressing the 1933 Winnats meeting. Bert Ward is on the extreme front left, along with Stephen Morton (with pipe) and Geoffrey Manders MP (with stick).

CHAPTER SEVEN

The future

As the years pass, constant problems arise. Very early on, the Kinder Scout Advisory Committee met a threat from a mining consortium which had been granted a licence by the Government to explore for oil on Kinder. The site for the proposed exploration was the Kinder Downfall.

We jumped into action and started a public campaign of opposition together with the Peak Park Board, the National Trust, Derbyshire County Council and of course the bodies represented on the Advisory Committee. The appropriate Government Ministers were approached, the mining consortium itself was contacted, MPs were brought into the picture and we were successful in fending off the threat.

We are not under any illusions that this could not be attempted again. Constant vigilance is required to see to it that this does not happen.

After that, another threat arose. The Conservative Government issued an instruction to Water Authorities that they should sell off surplus catchment land. Not only would this have been a threat to water purity from farmers using excessive nitrates on land with leaching into streams, and doing the same with herbicides, pesticides and other poisons, it would also threaten any Water Authority footpaths existing on sold-off land.

The Government was very clear that such 'restrictions' would not automatically apply on catchment land sold. This threat also applied to any possible sale of Forestry Commission land. A new threat then arose in the privatisation of Water Authorities. The Ministry of Defence too was advised to increase its land holdings, and battles on this issue were already taking place in some areas.

Finally the greatest challenge for centuries faces us in the countryside. Following on the food surplus problems created by the Common Agricultural policy, it was proposed by the Government that upwards of 5,000,000 acres of farmland should be taken out of production

We PLEDGE our lifelong intent to regard ourselves at liberty, in exercise of the simple human freedoms which we rightly claim, to walk with our families and friends for recreation of body and mind wherever public access to open country is presently allowed by the water authorities. We shall cause no damage, break no criminal law, neither threaten nor commit any violence nor intrude upon anybody's privacy. But if free access to these lands is at any time denied we now declare that the threat of legal action for trespass, which is not a criminal offence, shall not deter us from exercising our traditional right of access to the hills. Rivington, 7th May 1989.

Benny was secretary of the Rivington Pledge Committee which campaigned against the barring of public right of access to Water Authority land, in the Water Privatisation Bill

GLORIA GAFFNEY

Benny and Don Lee in 1989

Benny speaking at the Rivington Rally in May 1989

for 'other' uses. What these uses were was the subject of much debate. We must be on our guard to see that no development is allowed in the countryside without full monitoring by planning bodies representing not only farmers and landowners, but ordinary people and leisure bodies.

I am confident that we will face up to the problems and struggles to protect our heritage from ruin as we have always done. The battles ahead are not only for access but for the conservation of the countryside.

Benny Rothman wrote this additional chapter in 1987 for a planned new edition of the book which was never published. This updated version is reproduced by kind permission of the Rothman family.

Benny, Gloria Gaffney and Benny's wife Lily

Above top: The 1970 BBC reconstruction of the Trespass in William Clough with Benny Rothman, followed by Dave Nesbitt, Ewan MacColl and Tona Gillett.

Above right: Benny and Martin Doughty at the opening of the Midshires Way in 1994.

Right: Three veteran countryside campaigners - (left to right) Benny, Tom Stephenson and Stephen Morten at National Park rally in Cave Dale.
This is a rare photograph of Benny and Tom together as they did not agree on the significance of the 1932 trespass nor some of the facts about it.

Benny opening the new National Trust path to Kinder, April 1985

Life after prison

After serving his prison sentence at Leicester, Benny Rothman embarked on a career in the engineering industry, both as a worker and union leader. The 1932 Trespass was never forgotten and the BBC's 'Look Stranger' reconstruction of the protest in 1970 was seen by many. Books such as Crichton Porteous' 'Peakland' (1954), Roly Smith's 'First and Last' published by The Peak National Park (1978), and Keith Warrender's 'High Peak Faces and Places' (1978) brought the subject to new generations.

By 1979, Benny was campaigning against government countryside legislation. With the publicity surrounding the 50th Anniversary Trespass celebrations and the

1986 CND mass trespass at Coulport

publication of his account of the protest, Benny became much involved in other campaigns for access. In September 1990 at the age of 79, he led a group over a four-mile route on Snailsden Moor, South Yorkshire. The following year he took part in a protest, along with Mike Harding, on a common land dispute, close to Prime Minister John Major's home in Huntingdon.

He was once again trespassing in July 1991 when he took part in a walk over Thurlstone Moor which had been closed off to the public by a shooting syndicate. Benny stated he was prepared for prison again if necessary, because he believed the people's right of access was being gradually eroded.

Benny was secretary of both the Kinder Scout Advisory Committee, and the Rivington Pledge Committee, which was in the forefront in the fight against privatisation of water authority property. He was credited with helping to win concessions in water privatisation legislation.

Benny was also involved in protests against military use of Holcombe Moor, Bury and at Coulport, Loch Long. He was made an honorary life member of the Ramblers' Association in 1996 and, after his death, a mountain in Greenland was named after him.

Ironically, a public footpath at the side of Benny's house in Crofton Avenue, Timperley, Cheshire was threatened with closure. Following a vigorous campaign the right of way was saved in 1995. Now supporters are hoping to put a blue plaque on his old home.   (KW)

Big names and big deeds on Kinder

By Tom Waghorn

Eighty years after the controversial Mass Trespass by those idealist young Manchester ramblers on April 24, 1932, some of the facts are still disputed.

How many took part? Exactly how far did they get on Kinder Scout? Was there really a 'battle'? What was the route of the Sheffield contingent√ Did those arrested get a fair trial?

In this updated version of Benny Rothman's Mass Trespass book of 30 years ago, we've tried to answer some of those questions, including featuring the views of one of the gamekeepers involved.

It hasn't been easy. One of the golden rules of journalism is to beware of referring to something as the 'first' or 'only' or 'last'. I broke the rule when I wrote in the Manchester Evening News that Jimmy Jones, the 'last' of the trespassers had been tragically killed in a road accident near his home in Northenden.

Clang! A phone call from an old lady, Edith Stringer, insisted that she was one of the protesters on that perfect, fine day.

So what happened to them all? Woolfie Winnick, Benny's lieutenant, became a successful businessman, in contrast to the lifelong struggles of his leader.

There are 24 boxes of cuttings and records of Benny's activities at the Working Class Movement Library in Salford. Ask the helpful librarians and they'll produce the notes, written in blue ink, which Benny compiled in his unlit prison cell for his defence at the trial.

After serving his sentence in Leicester jail the 21year-old Rothman found himself on the dole in the leanest years of the Great Depression. He believed that he had been put on an employers' blacklist. And the fact that he was a Communist could not have helped.

Eventually he turned his back on the motor trade and found a job at AV Roe's aircraft factory. Then, around the 1950s, he was at Metro-Vicks in the sprawling Trafford Park, reputedly the world's biggest industrial estate.

A machine-tool fitter, he became a shop steward, serving on the works committee with one of the great militant union leaders, Hugh (later Lord) Scanlon, affectionately known as 'Scannie'. Terry Perkins, former chairman of Greater Manchester and High Peak Ramblers' Association, worked at the company at the same time. 'Benny won the reputation of getting the best piecework rates for his fellow engineers,' recalls Terry. 'This was not to the liking of his employers and they sacked him. His workmates did not lift a finger to oppose this victimisation and they let him go through the door'.

Benny Rothman signing copies of the first edition of the book in 1982 at the Bookline bookshop Altrincham with owner Robert Elman

Jimmy's tale

Jimmy Jones was fifteen when he took part in the protest. When I chatted with him in 2002 he had few recollections of the event, except that he had been invited to come by Benny Rothman whom he had met at the Young Communist League. Being a young teenager he felt on the fringe of things and did not remember any direct involvement with keepers.

He had wanted to study pharmacy but was turned down because his dad was a labourer, but was later offered an apprenticeship in engineering.

Jimmy continued to campaign for ramblers' rights throughout his life. He was very active into old age and showed me his darts and bowls trophies, and was also involved in a local protest against mobile phone masts in his neighbourhood. He died after being knocked down in a road accident in 2003. (KW)

Benny lived at Timperley with wife Lily (they met at a peace camp as young people), tended his allotment and did any amount of community work. Membership of Altrincham and Sale Trades Council was just one of his activities.

He was a brilliant and emotive speaker at access rallies and lost count of the number of times he was taken back to 'the scene of the crime' on Kinder by TV companies.

Bernard Rothman (Benny was a childhood nickname) suffered a stroke at 85, which immobilised him physically but not mentally. He died in 2002, aged 90, a year after Lily. His ashes, if I remember rightly, were scattered not on Kinder but on Bleaklow.

One of the curious points about the 24 April demonstration is that a few of the protesters became national or international personalities. The young Jimmie Miller, for instance, changed his name to Ewan MacColl. Obstinate, egotistical and obsessed with politics, his fame as the 'King of Folkies' derived essentially from his songs.

He died in 1989, aged 74. His third wife, Peggy Seeger, and three of his children were there when his ashes were fed to the winds on Bleaklow.

A promising young musician, Michael Tippett, was staying with a Manchester Guardian reporter, David Ayerst, that weekend. He went along to Hayfield with his friend, who was

covering the protest for his newspaper. Tippett went on ahead of Ayerst and was hit on the hand by a stone thrown by a gamekeeper and had to go back for first-aid. The pair were only saved from being arrested by Ayerst showing his Press pass.

It was the deep divisions in society and mass unemployment of the times that inspired his memorable oratorio, A Child of Our Time. I recall reading Sir Michael Tippett's mention of his part in the Trespass in a Hallé programme when Manchester staged a festival of his music more than 20 years ago.

Benny and Lily

The distinguished historian AJP Taylor, then a lecturer at Manchester University, also strode out with the protesters. He is believed to have been the only academic involved, his students having been threatened with expulsion from the university if they went to Hayfield.

In his autobiography A Personal History, Taylor tells how a group of academics managed at least one all-day walk each weekend on Kinder or Bleaklow. The trespassers included Reginald Eastwood (Professor of English Law) and Louis Mordell (Professor of Pure Mathematics).

Taylor tells how Eastwood made a Manchester University party creep along under a wall for half a mile because gamekeepers were watching for them. It turned out that Reg was playing a prank on another professor who was with them, who was 'extremely law-abiding'.

Edith's tale

Edith Stringer used to be thought of as the oldest surviving member of the Trespass. She was eleven when she was taken with her brother Walter and sister Nelly. They travelled by train from their home in Miles Platting to Hayfield where they often went camping.

She was terrified when she got to the village because she saw a notice attached to a tree that warned that trespassers would be prosecuted and thought that she would go to prison. Edith later went to live in Chorlton and often told her children about that exciting if scary day.   (KW)

MANCHESTER EVENING NEWS

Most intriguing of all, the events of April 24 even spawned a musical. The multi-talented Mike Harding created *A Free Man on Sunday* performed by Manchester Youth Theatre at New Mills town hall for the 60th anniversary. It was the same town hall where Benny and his friends appeared in the magistrates' court before being sent for trial at Derby. There were other mass trespasses, of course, though Kinder proved to be the most crucial. One wonders what would have happened if those determined young ramblers hadn't been sent to jail...

DERBYSHIRE CONSTABULARY
SECTION STATION

MASS TRESPASS ON KINDER SCOUT
APRIL 24th 1932

The six ramblers arrested on this trespass were kept locked up in the cells of this police building before being tried at Derby Assizes. It is now accepted that the Mass Trespass helped to bring about the Act of Parliament which established the National Parks and Access to the Countryside.

Benny Rothman unveiling the commemorative plaque at New Mills police station, March 1994.

65

Behind the Trespass

By Keith Warrender

Here are the experiences of three young men connected with the Mass Trespass. Two of them had known nothing about the protest as they began their day. But it was to end with painful memories - for different reasons, as they were caught up in it. The other knew all about the planned action, but made sure he did not suffer the consequences.

The greatest injustice?

John Anderson received the longest sentence of six months for his part in the Trespass and yet for the rest of his life protested his innocence. He wrote to me in 1981 outlining his version of events. He was then 70 years old and was scared that the letter would get him into more trouble. Even in 1994 at the ceremony to unveil a plaque to the trespassers outside New Mills police station, Anderson grabbed the microphone to restate his belief that he had been ill-treated. 'At last I am able to state my innocence' he shouted, 'Those who accused me of attacking a game keeper are trained liars'. His outcry is reported to have received the biggest cheer at the ceremony.

Had he received 'rough justice' or was he in denial of his role during that eventful day? He had set off on the morning of the Trespass from his home in Droylsden to walk from Hayfield via William Clough to Glossop. When he got to Hayfield he mingled with the protesters and was photographed with them in his cap and distinctive khaki drill jacket with breast pockets and brass buttons. Plain-clothes police would surely have spotted him and presumed he was one of the trespassers. When the marchers set off, he tagged along at the rear and got into conversation with Sol Gadian who was part of the official march. It soon became clear to Sol that Anderson was totally against the protest and remembered him saying 'How would you like someone to go through your garden? I am going to help the gardeners.'

KEITH WARRENDER

Anderson then walked with W Hanley, a rambler who was also against the Trespass. As the main group broke off at William Clough, Anderson, Hanley and others sat on a slope to watch the events unfold. They saw scuffles break out between the gamekeepers and the crowd. As a keeper was beaten to the ground, Anderson rushed to his aid. He got closely involved in the fighting and Tona Gillett, thinking Anderson was on his side called out to him 'Do you need any help?'

It was wrongly assumed by the witness that he was referring to the stricken keeper, Edward Beever and so Anderson was arrested for assault. His companions protested against the arrest but were threatened with the same if they did not back off.

Anderson's defence at the trial was that he had neither hit nor struggled with Beever. Unfortunately, witnesses who could have testified he was against the protest, did not turn up. He had been unwise to be photographed with the trespassers

Anderson's involvement was noted by a police witness and he had been seen in the melee with his fist clenched. He was easy to identify and moments later was overheard saying, possibly to Hanley, 'He should have kept his xxxx hands off!'

Opposite: Trespasser Sol Gadian at the 1982 reunion.
Above: John Anderson (left) in his distinctive jacket and Lance Helman.
Below: L-R (front) Martin Doughty leader of Derbyshire County Council, Benny Rothman. (Middle) Arthur Schofield, Jimmy Jones, Bella Costello, unknown, John Anderson. (Back) Harry Rowley(?), George Sumner, John Simmonds, outside New Mills police station, 1994.

and should have restrained himself when he saw the keeper being assaulted. If he had been able to call upon Sol Gadian and Hanley, the outcome of the trial would surely have been different for him.

However, Anderson was able to draw great satisfaction at the ceremony to honour the Trespass veterans at New Mills in 1994. Derbyshire's Chief Constable, who was also present, publicly agreed that Anderson was innocent of the charges. After so many years of hurt, Anderson described it as 'a happy day'.

Division amongst the trespassers

The seeming injustice of Anderson's situation was further heightened by the actions of some the Trespass organisers. Lance Helman surprisingly wrote to the Manchester Evening News in 1982, prior to the 50th Trespass anniversary celebrations, describing how he dodged arrest. Lance was in the group of ramblers photographed with John Anderson as they set off, and he is seen standing with Benny Rothman as he addressed the ramblers in the quarry.

KEITH WARRENDER

Lance Helman in 1982

But Lance disappeared after the Trespass. I am not sure whether he had discussed it with his fellow marchers, but in a premeditated act, he made sure he was not arrested. Rather than walking back into Hayfield, he went with a group which included 'Woolfie' Winnick - Benny Rothman's friend and minder - via Doctor's Gate

and then went down to Little Hayfield and through to Marple. At some point when it was safe to stop, he changed out of his walking gear into flannel trousers and an old raincoat, before boarding a train at Marple. To make sure he did not run into any police waiting for him at London Road (now Piccadilly) Station, he alighted at Ashburys Station and made his way home undetected.

Lance was Secretary of the Ramblers' Rights Movement at the time, but he must have decided it was not worth losing his job or facing the authorities and so he and others left Benny and his friends to face the consequences. Inevitably this put a strain on the friendships between those who spent time in prison and the people who escaped punishment. Ironically, donations of financial support for the imprisoned ramblers had to be sent to Lance as Secretary of the organisation.

Lance has since done something for which we should be grateful. He very kindly agreed to the use of his rare set of press photos in the first edition of this book. Lance had presumably bought them because he is seen in at least three of them. Without these iconic images our understanding of those who took part and what happened would be diminished.

Caught up in the violence

Edward Beever, the keeper, was not the only person to be beaten up on the day of the Trespass. Beever was taken to hospital in Stockport after the incident and, thankfully, according to a press report, was discharged the same day. It has been suggested by some that he died from the injuries he received, but they obviously did not realise that he gave evidence in court a few weeks later.

George Elliot wrote to me in 1981 following my appeal for more information about the Trespass, prior to the first edition of this book. He was a member of the Fell and Rock Climbing Club and lived in Preston.

His letter was a reminder that the violence on the day was not just from the protesters. He was eighteen at the time and had spent the previous night in a cave at Laddow Rocks. The next morning he set off to walk over Kinder on his way to Goyt Valley. As he crossed the Kinder plateau he came across an unusual scene. There was a line of gamekeepers with their backs to him, and beyond them a large crowd of people. He sensed this seemed to be a trouble spot and tried to alter his route. He was spotted by some of the trespassers who cheered him thinking he was part of the protest. Elliot innocently waved back, but now the keepers had noticed him and approached him.

He quite expected to be rough-handled, but was not prepared for the flourish of punches that knocked him to the ground as he tried to defend himself. Elliot's recollections were rather hazy after that, but he did recall ramblers coming over to help him. He remembered lots of shouting and cheering and 'people swarming over the place'. Other hikers were praising him for creating a diversion to allow the trespassers to move forward. But he felt confused, not only from the punches, but trying to fathom out what he was supposed to have done!

Half-dazed, he continued his walk down to the Goyt Valley. It was only when he later read the papers that he realised he had been caught up in a protest for the right of access. Ironically, Elliot got to know many of the moors gamekeepers quite well. In 1939 there was an appeal for people who knew their way around areas such as Kinder to patrol at night to look out for enemy parachutists. It meant that former 'adversaries', keepers and hikers, were working together.

'I remember the many trespasses we made across Kinder and Bleaklow, only four or five of us at a time. Sometimes we made it across. Other times we met gamekeepers who tried to push us back the way we had come. Believe me, being struck across bare legs in winter time is no joke. '

Letter to the Manchester Evening News

As they chatted during the early hours, it became clear that some of the keepers quite enjoyed the cat-and-mouse game of the trespassing walkers as they tried to outwit them - providing there was no violence or damage. Despite the bruising encounter on the day of the Trespass, Elliot still remembers the kindness of many gamekeepers whom he later met.

Elliot became a rock-climber and an enthusiast for the fells and crags of the Lake District. He took part in the first ascents of climbs on Bowfell and Pavey Ark, above Langdale, between 1942 and 1943. (TW)

From Flamenco to fences

By Roly Smith

When the Peak District National Park was set up just over 60 years ago - on April 17, 1951 - it was significant that one of the first jobs it did was to negotiate access agreements with landowners on the former battle-grounds of the 1930s.

The first-ever access agreement allowing walkers their long-cherished freedom to roam was signed just a year later, and covered 5,780 acres of the southern slopes of Kinder Scout and Broadlee Bank Tor. By the time of the passing of the CROW Act in 2000, more than 90 square miles of Peak District moorland were covered by such agreements, under which the landowner was paid an annual sum to allow walkers free access, apart from the few days every year when shooting was taking place.

Perhaps because of its history as being in the cockpit of the access movement, the Peak District had to be the national front-runner in the negotiation of access agreements, which were available to all local authorities under the provisions of the 1949 National Parks and Access to the Countryside Act. In fact, 80 per cent of the access agreements in the entire country were eventually found in the Peak District.

The access agreements on the northern moors also gave rise to the first-ever ranger service - although they were then known as wardens - in any British national park. Landowners considered it important that the park instituted some kind of policing of visitors on these newly opened-up areas.

KEITH WARRENDER

It was on a bright Easter Monday morning in April, 1954, that the Peak District National Park's warden service was inaugurated, the chairman of the county council standing on an upturned beer crate outside the Nag's Head in Edale to make the announcement. That was ironic because the first-ever full-time warden was Tom Tomlinson, a lifelong teetotaller from Rossendale, Lancashire.

Tom's test for becoming a new warden was typical of the man, according to former Chief Ranger, Ken Drabble. 'You had to go out with Tom and follow him straight up the Nab on the southern edge of Kinder. If you kept up with him (and he had an enormously long stride) and could answer a question at the top, you were accepted. If you were still struggling up the slope, he'd ask you to come back when you were fit.'

Indisputably, the Mass Trespass on Kinder in1932 had brought the access issue to a head, and acted as an important catalyst to the whole National Parks and access to the countryside campaign which eventually led to the legislation 17 years later by the post-war Labour Government.

Above: Grindslow Knoll. Top: The Woolpacks, Kinder.

Even so, huge tracts of moorland still remained inaccessible to the public for another 50 years until the passing of the Countryside and Rights of Way (CROW) Act in 2000, and its final implementation in 2005. Again, the Peak District National Park was the first to embrace the new legislation, and it set up a Local Access Forum under the Act in December, 2000.

As a result of the CROW Act, the public's right of access to open country in the Peak District National Park increased from one quarter to one third. The actual figures show it went up from 92 square miles to 193 square miles (240 sq km to almost 500 sq km).

The 'Right to Roam' Act was seen by most as the culmination of the efforts of those brave

71

'Although I was only 12 years old when it happened, I have always been very influenced by the Mass Trespass. I am still horrified both by the attitude of landowners at the time, who included my grandfather, the 9th Duke, in not allowing people to walk in open country, and by the vicious sentences handed down to the trespassers.'

The 11th Duke of Devonshire speaking at the 2002 Trespass rally

trespassers, although sadly few lived to see its enactment. Benny Rothman, for example, died at the age of 90 in January 2002.

The National Trust acquired 3,860 acres of the Hayfield Estate on the western side of Kinder Scout, including the scene of the Trespass, for £600,000 in September, 1982. Financial support for the Trust's bid was received from the then Countryside Commission and the National Heritage Memorial Fund. The Trust's policy of allowing inalienable free access to its open country properties gave walkers the freedom of Kinder at last.

Since then, the Trust has acquired the whole of the Kinder and Bleaklow plateaux, as well as most of the farms in Edale. It has also undertaken an extensive programme of moor-land restoration on Kinder. This has included the banning of sheep grazing and the removal of an astonishing 38,000 'bandit' sheep in the first 20 years of its ownership. Restoration work

has included the re-wetting and re-seeding of large areas of peat moorland, in conjunction with the Moors for the Future Partnership.

Various celebrations have been held over the years to commemorate the Mass Trespass, as it seems to be a story which will never die. Secretary of State for the Environment Michael Meacher attended the 70th anniversary event at Bowden Bridge, Hayfield in 2002, when the show was stolen by the late 11th Duke of Devonshire who, showing great dignity, apologised for the attitudes of landowners, including his own grandfather, in 1932.

And at the 75th anniversary in 2007, the then Environment Secretary and later Foreign Secretary David Miliband, after unveiling the name of a train at Manchester's Piccadilly station in honour of Benny Rothman, announced the Labour Government's intention to proceed with access provision to the 6,000 miles of the British coastline.

In August 2009, a group of 40 members of the A Desalambrar Spanish walking group followed the Mass Trespass route to Kinder Scout, led by local walkers. Based in the Andalusian city of Cordoba in southern Spain, A Desalambrar are fighting the same fight against intractable landowners as Benny Rothman and his companions did 80 years ago in Derbyshire. When they reached Kinder Low, they astonished their English hosts by breaking into the vigorous hand-clapping and syncopated rhythms of the flamenco!

Later the same year. Kinder Scout was declared the 223rd National Nature Reserve in the country by Natural England, in recognition of its 'iconic social and environmental importance.' It was also dedicated to the memory of Sir Martin Doughty, the New Mills man and lover of Kinder Scout whose father had been on the Trespass. Martin became chairman of the county council and the National Park and later of Natural England, before his untimely death from cancer earlier in the year.

In 2010, the National Trust announced plans to fence-off just over five square miles of Kinder's 2,088ft summit with a 12 mile-long fence. But this time it was not to keep out ramblers, but Kinder's notoriously voracious grazing sheep, which had been recognised as one of the main reasons for Kinder's lack of re-vegetation.

The fence is temporary, and there are multiple access points for walkers. It surrounds the most eroded parts of Kinder and gives plants like heather, bilberry and cotton grass the chance to take root. In the meantime, a five-year, £2.5 million programme of restoration by gully-blocking, brash spreading and

Top: David Miliband, Secretary of State for the Environment at the unveiling of the train named after Benny at Piccadilly Station Manchester, along with Benny's son Harry and great grandchildren Isabella and Harvey, in 2007.

Left: Martin Doughty, Tom Levitt MP for High Peak, and David Miliband at New Mills in 2007.

re-vegetation is being carried out inside the fence, in an attempt to restore Kinder to its former glory.

In 2011, Hayfield Parish Council announced plans for a Trespass Heritage Centre in the centre of the village from where the trespassers set off in 1932. Ironically, the site planned for the new centre was in the former village lock-up in Dungeon Brow, where Benny Rothman and the other arrested trespassers were first incarcerated 80 years before. The centre had received over £100,000 in funding from the Heritage Lottery Fund, the Peak District National Park Authority, and the National Trust, but a change in the composition of the elected members of the parish council resulted in a decision to abandon the centre, and the grant money was handed back.

However, the Independent Kinder Visitor Centre Group then set up the Kinder Trespass Archive Project. The intention is that photographs, memorabilia and memories of the event and surrounding issues will be made available on a dedicated website. The long term aim is still to establish a visitor centre in Hayfield to display some of this material and to be a focus for access issues today.

There can be little doubt that the Kinder Trespass of 1932 has now entered the realms of the mythology of the outdoor movement, giving its perpetrators a totally unsought aura of martyrdom. But equally, as ramblers now enjoy the unparalleled sense of freedom which is provided by the tors, groughs and cloughs of Kinder Scout, it is a story which should never be allowed to be forgotten.

The 1990 Spanish visit to Kinder

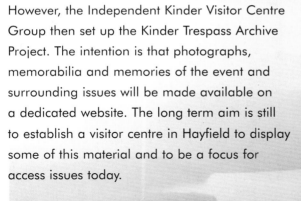

Kinder Reservoir from Sandy Heys

Milestones on the path to freedom

1865 Commons and Open Spaces Society formed

1876 Hayfield and Kinder Scout Ancient Footpaths Association formed

1884 Liberal MP James Bryce introduces first Access to Mountains Bill

1893 Co-operative Holidays Association formed by TA Leonard for rambling holidays

1894 The Peak & Northern Footpaths Society formed in Manchester

1900 Sheffield Clarion Ramblers founded by GHB Ward - the first working class rambling club

1905 First Federation of Rambling Clubs formed in London

1932 Mass Trespass on Kinder Scout; five ramblers imprisoned

1935 Ramblers' Association founded

1938 Access to Mountains Bill introduced by Arthur Creech-Jones, becoming the severely emasculated and largely unused Access to Mountains Act of 1939

1945 Rambler and architect John Dower produces his report on national parks

1949 National Parks and Access to the Countryside Act passed, allowing access agreements with landowners

1951 Peak District becomes the first national park and negotiates access agreements to Kinder Scout the following year. Sixty per cent of access agreements are in the Peak

1965 Tom Stephenson's Pennine Way long distance path opens, crossing Kinder Scout and Bleaklow

2000 Countryside and Rights of Way Act passed, enshrining the right of walkers to roam freely in open country

2001 First access forums set up   (RS)

The gamekeeper's tale

In 1982 my father, John Watson, was contacted by the BBC and invited to attend a broadcast with Benny Rothman. He refused as he did not wish to be involved with any publicity for the book which Benny was preparing for the 50th anniversary of the Trespass.

He was not aware that the BBC were recording the conversation. Parts of this were later broadcast without his permission and extracts were taken out of context. He was very annoyed with the BBC and decided to write the following account about the event.

Ian Watson

The 'mythical Mass Trespass'

'For several weeks newspapers had announced that a Mass Trespass over Kinder Scout would take place, led by members of the British Workers' Sports Federation. These were mostly young communists from around the Manchester area and, I presume, readers of The Daily Worker.

On April 24, 1932 a meeting of ramblers took place at Hayfield. A few hundred were present but the organisers were disappointed as they had expected thousands. Nevertheless, they went on to Bowden Bridge where the leaders addressed the gathering in the quarry and discussed which way to approach Kinder. They decided to walk up the public road to the reservoir and then follow the public footpath up and around to William Clough. By this time the crowd had dwindled to about 100 or 150.

Part way up the clough some of the hikers left the path for about 50 yards, where they were met by two gamekeepers and ten local farmers, etc., who had volunteered to help. A short scuffle took place and one of the men, Edward Beevers, was kicked in the groin. Whilst he lay on the ground four 'brave' people lay on his arms and legs to hold him down. A farmer, Fred Simpson, picked them off one by one and threw them down the heathery bank.

John Watson

A whistle was then blown (a pre-arranged signal) and all the so-called 'mass' trespassers returned to the public footpath. Here the majority of the hikers decided to return to Hayfield while others, who had not participated in the 'trespass,' continued up the clough footpath. At Hayfield, police who were dressed as hikers and had accompanied the walkers to William Clough, identified the six ringleaders to uniformed officers and these were arrested. So the whole 'Mass Trespass' consisted of about 50 yards by 100 yards wide.

It was claimed by these people that a large party walked from Edale across Kinder Scout via Kinder Downfall and joined this party at William Clough. This statement was quite untrue, because I was there with another 16 men on the ridge near the Downfall (Sandy Heys) with the whole area in view for the full day, and nobody crossed Kinder that day. What actually happened was that two groups met on the public footpath at Ashop Head. The group who had witnessed the incident from the William Clough path (some of these may have been the party who walked from Edale via Edale Cross) met another group, who had walked up the footpath from the Woodlands Valley at Ashop Head. Gamekeepers from the Woodlands Valley had kept this later group under observation to ensure that they stayed on the public footpath.

This stupid episode caused much concern with the genuine walker and did more harm than good. For several weeks after this incident, members of the Ramblers' Federation, the Rucksack Club and Bogtrotters looked me up to offer their hand and apologise. Any claims that this affair helped to bring about Access to Mountains are complete fallacy, as this Bill had been going back and forth in various forms for over 50 years. Then, when national parks were first considered for selected parts of Britain, someone had the bright idea of joining the two Bills into one - ie The National Parks and Access to Mountains Bill. So when one Bill passed so did the other. Why this senseless and stupid affair warrants so much publicity in the papers and television and a plaque fixed in the quarry to the memory of the mythical 'Mass Trespass' is beyond comprehension!

I was head gamekeeper (succeeding my father, Peter Watson) and estate manager on Kinder Estate, owned by James Watts, for many years so I am one of only a few local people who

know the true facts about this over-publicised and grossly-exaggerated disturbance. I have read many of the accounts about the 'Mass Trespass' and they are getting more exaggerated with time.'

'Soon we turned to the left and continued along the hillside towards Ashop Head... Before we regained the footpath a halt was made for tea, and the Manchester contingent was joined by a party of about thirty from Sheffield, who had marched from Hope over Jacob's Ladder, from the top of which they had watched the battle with the keepers.'

Extract from the Guardian newspaper's eye-witness account by reporter David Ayerst who saw the Sheffield group join the trespassers.

The keepers and the Sheffield contingent

Ramblers of the pre-access days had a love-hate relationship with some of the keepers. John Watson, for instance, was affectionately known as 'the bloody Scotsman' and his golden labrador as 'the Yellow Peril'. Over at the Snake, in later years Joe Townsend was notorious for trying to scrounge Sunday papers from the walkers who had tramped up Doctor's Gate from Glossop.

The late Bill Keen, one of the Sheffield ramblers who took part in the protest, contradicted John Watson's account of the day. 'After catching the morning train to Edale, the ramblers walked over Jacob's Ladder to the Downfall, not encountering

any gamekeepers on the way,' he insisted in an interview. After meeting the Manchester lads 'we had to set off back across Kinder so we didn't miss the last train back to Sheffield'. The Sheffield part of the protest was also recorded in the Guardian (see above).

As for accounts of the Trespass getting more exaggerated, Benny Rothman never wavered from his original report of the Trespass and the aftermath. Also we have the original press reports of the protest and trial which generally tally with Benny's version.

Tom Waghorn

GAMEKEEPERS AND GROUSE MOORS

THE other day a letter appeared in one of the leading dailies in which an Oldhamer told how roughly he and a few friends had been stopped by a gamekeeper on a local moor. He did not give the name of the moor, but I know one where I am told the gamekeeper does not know his job. I cannot imagine what harm or damage two or three men can do in walking over a rain-sodden moor in winter. But there are gamekeepers not over intelligent who think it a part of their duty to try and put the fear of death into a man for merely going a few yards on a moor.

For years I spent all my spare time and all my holidays on the moors from Black Hill, beyond Isle of Skye, and the White House of Blackstone Edge—I was gathering material for the book I published on local prehistoric sites. I knew all the gamekeepers, seven or eight, on that long stretch of moorland, and I never had any trouble with them, but I knew other men who had been bullied and cursed out of all reason. One day I sat with a gamekeeper by a moorland road when two young men came down the moor. The gamekeeper stopped them and when he had done cursing he said that they would have to go to Huddersfield Police Court.

When they had gone I said, " You might have spoken more quietly to those men and warned them. You have made enemies, and what is to stop them from coming here some hot day and finding you weeks of hard work?"

"How can they do it?" he asked. I told him and he said, "I had never thought of that; I wonder if it has been done?"

"I think it has," I said, "for it is so easy for a man to get more than his own back out of a gamekeeper. Men do not like being bullied for nothing."

There is something to be said for the gamekeeper. We should not forget that he is a working man, who is expected to earn his wages. People should not go over the moors in the nesting season. Some gamekeepers rarely go on their moors at that time, for they know that the best breeding results are obtained when the birds are not disturbed.

No one should take a dog on the moors when grouse are sitting. I have known them to forsake their eggs when they have been flushed off the nest by a dog. In my spring roaming I kept to the high bare ground till the young broods were well on the wing.

When the owner of a moor brings his friends for the August shoot, and few birds are found, the sport is poor. Then he wants to know why they are scarce, and what his gamekeeper has been doing. If it had been a wet, stormy nesting time, he has a good answer, but if the spring had been dry and mild his answers are not always accepted as satisfactory. Then there are poachers to watch, and vermin to keep down, so that a gamekeeper's life is not without its trials, yet for all that he need not be so roughspoken to a man who is out on a moor for nothing but a walk.

Mr. G. H. B. Ward, in his little booklet, says, "There is no time for trespass but only for proven damage done. No damage can be assessed for uncultivated fruits, bilberries, etc." The late Halliwell Sutcliffe said that if a rambler chanced to knock a fence down he should leave half a crown behind.

A. W.

Writer and poet Ammon Wrigley's letter to the Oldham Chronicle, February 1937

NATIONAL TELEPHONE 5003.

ESTATE & INSURANCE
AGENTS & BROKERS.

Princes Chambers.
19, Chapel Walks.

Manchester September 12th 1906

Arnold H. Doughty Esq,
My dear Sir

I much regret having to call your attention to the injury you no doubt thoughtlessly inflicted on my client Mr James Watts, the owner of Kinder Scout and the Downfall by climbing with ropes up the Downfall on Sunday last - I beg to call your attention to the fact that during the grouse or pheasant season any disturbance of the game is a very serious matter and detracts from the letting value of the moor as a sporting property -

a brace of birds which may only fetch 5/- or 6/- at a dealers may have cost the owner from £1 to £2 to rear per head according to the season. Bearing this in mind you will see it is not fair to disturb and frighten off the birds as you and your companions did in the middle of the season and just before a large party of shooting guests took the moor. I must therefore ask you to send me a note promising that you will not go again across the Moor - except of course on the recognised roads & oblige

Yrs Truly
Edward Neild
Agent to James Watts Esq

Holmfield
Normanton
by Derby -

1906 letter from Kinder Scout owner Watts' agent requiring climbers who had gone to Kinder Downfall to promise in writing not to go across his property again. Watts argued his business interests were being damaged by the disturbance of the grouse during the shooting season.

In March 1922 Watts banned all walkers from crossing Kinder Scout for at least eighteen months. This followed the deaths of two ramblers - one had collapsed near the Downfall. Hundreds of searchers had gone on to Kinder and Watts claimed they had damaged the grouse breeding grounds. His solicitors stated that the owner had previously overlooked the occasional presence of trespassers. They added that the way over Kinder was 'bad walking' and 'dangerous'.

For two years before the Mass Trespass a few friends and I from New Mills made many unsuccessful attempts to get to the Downfall. Early in January, 1931, snow fell for two days then froze solid. So my friend and I decided we would meet no opposition.

After two hours struggle through the snow, we reached the top. The magnificent sight that met us, the frozen Downfall glistening in the winter sunshine, was unforgettable, with Hayfield in the valley below. We stood spellbound for a while before continuing - over the plateau. We were stopped, however, by three keepers, and escorted, not to Hayfield, but to the Snake, miles out of our way.

Letter to the Manchester Evening News

Opposite: Kinder Downfall

Kinder Trespass
anniversaries and reunions

*Above and top right: walkers
on the route up to Kinder*

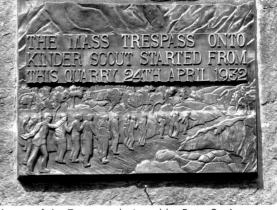

THE MASS TRESPASS ONTO
KINDER SCOUT STARTED FROM
THIS QUARRY 24TH APRIL 1932

50th Anniversary
1982

*Overleaf: The top of William Clough
during the 1982 Anniversary*

*Plaque of the Trespass designed by Peter Senior
unveiled at Bowden Bridge quarry*

PEAK DISTRICT NATIONAL PARK AUTHORITY

Above: Participants from the Trespass at the celebration

Alan Mattingly, Secretary of
The Ramblers, John Beadle,
chairman of the Peak Park,
and Benny Rothman

PEAK DISTRICT NATIONAL PARK AUTHORITY

PEAK DISTRICT NATIONAL PARK AUTHORITY

GLORIA GAFFNEY

On the first fine Sunday this summer, a large number of people gathered in a quarry in Derbyshire and sang a battle song (The Manchester Rambler). Its chorus startled the rooks and enchanted the onlookers.

The singers, most of whom have long ceased to be wage slaves, and many of whom can only ramble a step or two now, had gathered to celebrate the Kinder Trespass, the mass act of defiance which began in that same quarry on that same Sunday in April fifty six years ago. Twenty of the original trespassers were there with their friends and their relatives and with countless more of their contemporaries who had come to salute their achievement.

Beneath a permanent plaque which records that the Mass Trespass of Kinder Scout started from Bowden Bridge Quarry a mile out of Hayfield, the leader of the Trespass, Benny Rothman, who is a year or two short of eighty, and an inch or two short of five feet, is still a rambler on foot, but straight to the point in speech. Almost everyone in his audience already knew the story of that famous day (all ramblers do) but to hear it from Benny himself, standing there in breeches and yellow stockings, like something out of Shakespeare, was not only to recall it again but to re-live it.

Not that everyone among those assembled approved. Some think that the Trespass was a great irrelevance. They said so at the time and they argue with Benny to this day. It deflected attention, they say, from the serious business of negotiating access to the moorland countryside. But others, and I am one of them, think it must have concentrated minds wonderfully. It laid claim to a right, a right then denied but soon after to be conceded, at least in principle.

Above: Trespass veterans at the meeting
Top: Benny sets off from Hayfield on the walk
to the quarry with Trespass veteran Arthur Rowley

1988 reunion

All this was discussed after the outdoor rally in the quarry at an indoor rally in the pub, the Royal Hotel in Hayfield. Speaker after speaker applauded the original trespassers (who were modest and witty about their exploits) and then went on to categorise the threats to the countryside today, and the obstacles to access - indiscriminate planting of conifers, privatisation of water, inappropriate tourist developments. The young present repeated the old battle-cry: the right of access on foot to all open country, to protect rights of way and to protect the natural beauty of the countryside. The old agreed and showed themselves not content to settle for previous battles won... Forgive us our Trespass, said one old gentleman, with mock contrition. But he fooled no one.

Extract from Brian Redhead's 'Personal Perspectives' (Andrew Deutsch 1994). He was then a BBC Radio 4 presenter and president of the Council for National Parks

GLORIA GAFFNEY

Left to right: Speakers Jim Perrin, Alan Mattingly, Marion Shoard, Don Lee and Benny Rothman at the quarry rally

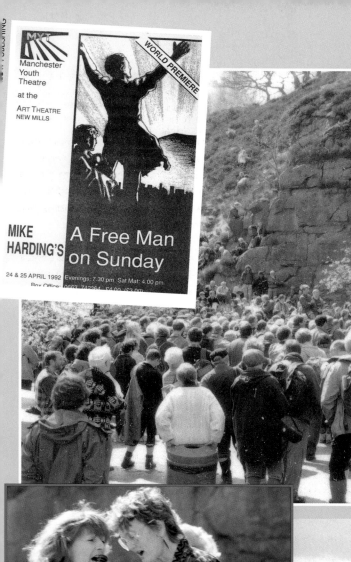

PEAK DISTRICT NATIONAL PARK AUTHORITY

60th Anniversary
1992

PEAK DISTRICT NATIONAL PARK AUTHORITY

Top: The celebrations included the premiere of Mike Harding's new play

Above: After a procession from Hayfield station car park there was a rally at Bowden Bridge quarry with speakers Ann Taylor MP, John Beadle, Chris Hall, Terry Howard and Benny Rothman. It finished with the singing of the 'Manchester Rambler' by Peggy Seeger and Irene Pyper Scott

Above: Trespass veterans left to right, Jimmy Jones, George Sumner, Benny Rothman and Bella Costello

87

The celebration was centred around a marquee at Bowden Bridge quarry with speakers Michael Meacher MP, Kate Ashbrook (Ramblers) and the Duke of Devonshire who gave his famous apology speech which welcomed ramblers onto his land. Mike Harding sang the 'Manchester Rambler', and Jim Perrin gave a moving tribute to Benny Rothman who had died a few months previously. Afterwards there was a walk up William Clough

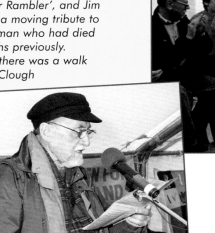

Terry Perkins, of Manchester Ramblers, friend and old union colleague of Benny Rothman

70th Anniversary
2002

That this House notes the 70th Anniversary of the Kinder Scout trespass on 24th April; recalls the commitment and bravery of Benny Rothman who led the trespass of 400 ramblers from Bowden Bridge Quarry, Hayfield, to the Kinder Scout mountain in the Peak District in 1932; believes this action laid the foundation of the campaign to gain access to mountain, moorland and other closed countryside in the UK; welcomes the passing of the Countryside and Rights of Way Act 2000 after decades of tireless campaigning by Benny Rothman and his supporters; expresses its deep sadness at his death in January; and notes that without his dedication and leadership thousands of square miles of British countryside could still remain closed to the public today.

Early day motion tabled by Tony Lloyd MP in March 2002 and signed by 119 other MPs

David Miliband, Environment Secretary in 2007, paid a glowing tribute to the 400 ramblers who 75 years ago exercised their right to roam on the Peak District moors, which later resulted in prison sentences for five of them.

Speaking at the 75th anniversary celebrations at New Mills, Mr Miliband said that without the action of the trespassers, the nation would not have the National Parks nor freedom to roam on mountain and moorland which the 22 million annual visitors to the Peak enjoy today.

He explained: 'We sometimes like to think that the thinking of politics is ahead of that of the people. There can be no doubt that in the 1930s, the politics were way behind the people, and the trespassers showed the way forward on access to moorland which is now enshrined in the Countryside and Rights of Way Act.'

Kate Ashbrook

Mr Miliband's speech was the keynote of a day of speeches, songs and stories centred on New Mills Town Hall, when about 300 ramblers from all over the country gathered to celebrate the anniversary.

Mike Harding

Other speakers at the New Mills event, compered by BBC Radio 2 folk show host Mike Harding, included Sir Martin Doughty, chair of Natural England, who came up with a Trespass Trail walking route based on New Mills. The trail was officially opened by Mr Miliband at the New Mills Heritage Centre by a sign which read 'Trespassers will be Celebrated - By Order'.

Lord Roy Hattersley, president of Friends of the Peak District; Kate Ashbrook, chair of the Ramblers' Association; Tony Hams, chair of the Peak District National Park authority and Jim Perrin, writer, access activist and friend of Benny Rothman, were the other speakers. There was also a 'work-in-progress' performance of a new community play 'On Common Ground', about the trespass, prior to a full performance later in the summer. The event concluded with a rousing rendition of Ewan MacColl's famous access anthem The Manchester Rambler.

75th Anniversary
2007

Throughout the weekend, guided walks led by National Park, Derbyshire County Council and National Trust rangers took many hundreds of walkers along part of the 14-mile Trespass Trail - including a 101-year-old lady who had travelled up from London for the event.   (RS)

Jim Perrin

'On Common Ground' by High Peak Community Arts

Lord Roy Hattersley

Kinder Scout close to the Downfall

Ewan MacColl

Music of moor and mountain

By Tom Waghorn

Ewan MacColl wrote more than 300 songs and three have survived to real significance in the 21st century. One is, perhaps, the most famous British folk song of all, *The Manchester Rambler*, plus *Dirty Old Town* (about Salford) and *The First Time Ever I Saw Your Face* (about his third-wife-to-be, Peggy Seeger).

That was in the late 1940s. The music of the people was performed everywhere by walkers and climbers in buses, trains, youth hostel common-rooms and campsites.. an essential part of the fun of being an outdoors type.

Some had their specialities. Joe Brown, for instance, Manchester's best-known and most adhesive cragsman, loved to perform *The Orderly Boom Opera*, a curiosity picked up from his soldiering days in Malaya, which linked army life to classical music. That was in the heyday of Manchester's Rock and Ice Club when climbers like Brown and Don Whillans were pioneering the hardest routes on Peak District gritstone and limestone.

But *The Manchester Rambler* remained the favourite. I heard it sung almost everywhere from a 1947 access-to-mountains rally in Cavedale at Castleton to a 21st birthday party at Leam Hall, the long-since-gone hostel near Grindleford. In those days there was no chorus, and today's chorus was then the first verse. 'Curly' Collier, a Stockport potholer, even had the effrontery to add two verses about caving to the ramblers' anthem!

MacColl's great angry protest song went around the world, popularised by top folk groups like The Spinners and The Dubliners. (I once, as a Mancunian, had the embarrassment of having to lead the singing with it at a rambling club gathering in Ireland).

It was even performed as a traditional loggers' song in a remote camp up Canada's Fraser River: *I'm a logger, I'm a logger from old B.C. way; I get all my pleasure by sweating all day. The Manchester Rambler* has become so absorbed into oral tradition that, 80 years on, many of the millions of modern ramblers may have lost sight of its origins. So how did it begin?

The popular version is that MacColl (then plain Jimmie Miller from Salford) wrote the words on Edale station while waiting for the Manchester train. It was some time in 1932, the singer-songwriter was then only 17 and the ballad was a spin-off from the Mass Trespass.

However, there's another version. Paul Craney, a Manchester folk-history expert, believed he remembered the very day Miller began to write his iconic song. Craney told me it was in early 1936, in one of Edale's two pubs, where their hiking party had been forced to retreat from Kinder, when the rain 'came down like stair-rods'.

In the party was Joan Littlewood, Miller's first wife, who with Miller was involved in an arts group staging politically-motivated plays in Manchester. As Joan, Paul and other theatre members were talking about the practicalities of putting on plays by Russian authors, Miller sat in a window seat, scribbling in a book.'We asked if he was writing a play, because he didn't do a lot of singing then,' recalled Mr Craney, 'but he said he was writing a song about ramblers. I'm sure it must have been *The Manchester Rambler*.

So, 1932 or 1936? Folk songs tend to change over the years, so both dates might have some link, perhaps with Craney's 1936 being a year or two earlier. The human memory can be fallible!

The words of *The Manchester Rambler* were pure, rebellious, radical Miller. Although he claimed to have written the jaunty little tune, some modern musicologists have insisted that it was taken from Haydn's 94th symphony. (No kidding! The Austrian wrote 104 symphonies and, in his younger days,

Peggy Seeger

Miller was interested in classical music).
And here's another odd thing. We all know the chorus:
I may be a wage slave on Monday,
But I am a free man on Sunday.

There were mutterings of disapproval in 1990 when a copy of the Bowden Bridge Trespass plaque was unveiled at Edale information Centre. Ewan and Peggy Seeger, in their later lives, had considered the words to be sexist and changed the hallowed phrase to *I have my freedom on Sunday*.

MacColl's song has survived partly because it deals with issues that are far broader than the Mass Trespass. One of his ditties, written before the April 2 protest, was popular at the time but has long since been forgotten. *The Trespass Song*, which used the tune of *The Road to the Isles*, went:

For by Kinder and by Bleaklow
and over the Goyt we go,
We'll ramble over mountain, moor and fen.
And we'll fight the trespass laws for every rambler's right,
And we'll ramble over Kinder once again.

I'll never forget the last time I heard *The Manchester Rambler* sung by the outdoors fraternity. It was July 10 2007 in the Rowan Chapel of Stockport Crematorium.

Nearly 100 of us - members and friends of Manchester's Karabiner Mountaineering Club - were saying goodbye to Len Stubbs, a founder of the club, a doughty long-distance moorland bogtrotter and one-time owner of shops in Manchester and Keswick.The KMC, like the song we were singing, began its existence at good old Edale. There were tears in some of our eyes as every one of us joined in *I've been over Snowdon, I've slept upon Crowden*. Ewan MacColl would certainly have approved!

93

The Manchester Rambler

Words and music by Ewan MacColl - press oficer on the Kinder Trespass

I've been over Snowdon, I've slept upon Crowden,
I've camped by the Wain Stores as well,
I've sun-bathed on Kinder, been burned to a cinder,
And many more things I can tell.
My rucksack has oft been my pillow,
The heather has oft been my bed,
And sooner than part from the mountains,
I think I would rather be dead.

CHORUS
I'm a rambler, I'm a rambler from Manchester way,
I get all my pleasure the hard moorland way,
I may be a wage slave on Monday,
But I am a free man on Sunday.

There's pleasure in dragging through peat bogs and bragging
Of all the fine walks that you know;
There's even a measure of some kind of pleasure
In wading through ten feet of snow.
I've stood on the edge of the Downfall,
And seen all the valleys outspread,
And sooner than part from the mountains,
I think I would rather be dead. (Cho.)

The day was just ending as I was descending
Through Grindsbrook just by Upper Tor,
When a voice cried, 'Hey, you!', in the way keepers do,
(He'd the worst face that ever I saw).
The things that he said were unpleasant;
In the teeth of his fury I said
That sooner than part from the mountains,
I think I would rather be dead. (Cho.)

He called me a louse and said 'Think of the grouse'.
Well, I thought but I still couldn't see
Why old Kinder Scout and the moors round about
Couldn't take both the poor grouse and me.
He said, 'All this land is my master's'.
At that I stood shaking my head,
No man has the right to own mountains
Any more than the deep ocean bed. (Cho.)

I once loved a maid, a spot-welder by trade,
She was fair as the rowan in bloom,
And the blue of her eye matched the June moorland sky,
And I loved her from April to June.
On the day that we should have been married,
I went for a ramble instead,
For sooner than part from the mountains,
I think I would rather be dead. (Cho.)

So I'll walk where I will over mountain and hill
And I'll lie where the bracken is deep,
I belong to the mountains, the clear running fountains
Where the grey rocks rise rugged and steep.
1 have seen the white hare in the gulleys,
And the curlew fly high overhead,
And sooner than part from the mountains
I think I would rather be dead. (Cho.)

The contributors

Roly Smith

Roly Smith is the author of over 70 books on the British country-side, and is president of the Outdoor Writers' and Photographers' Guild. He was recently described by a reviewer as 'one of Britain's most knowledgeable countryside writers.' Roly has long had a fascination with the Mass Trespass and the early battles for access, and has written extensively on the subject. He was privileged to know Benny Rothman as a personal friend, and firmly believes that the sacrifice that Benny and his friends made should never be forgotten.

Tom Waghorn

Tom Waghorn first met Benny Rothman while serving on the Committee which organised the 50th anniversary of the Mass Trespass. They remained firm friends until Benny's death. Tom was a former chief sub-editor, columnist and feature writer on the Manchester Evening News and has contributed to many out-door publications. He is a former vice-president of Manchester's Rucksack Club, a member of the Climbers' Club and a life member of National Union of Journalists.

Keith Warrender

Keith, a writer and publisher, has been giving talks on the Kinder Trespass for over thirty years. He first met Benny Rothman while researching his book 'High Peak Faces and Places' and then published Benny's account of the Trespass in 1982. During the preparation of the book, Benny, a near neighbour in Timperley, became a friend of the family. Keith is also a local historian and photographer and has written books about underground Manchester, and oddities around the region.

'Benny Rothman was well under five feet tall, a strong man, calm-eyed, watchful and humorous, with a passionate and selfless conviction'
JIM PERRIN

KEITH WARRENDER

Benny Rothman 1911-2002

The Moat Stones, the Woolpacks on the southern edge of Kinder

Acknowledgements

With thanks to

John Allen
Ida Bradshaw
June Cooper
Derbyshire Record Office
Ewan MacColl Ltd
Gloria Gaffney
Jan Gillett
Guardian newspaper
Mike Harding
Freda Irwin
Peter Jackson
Jo Kent
Don Lee
Raymond Leather
Gary Leigh
Manchester Evening News
Manchester County Record Office
Manchester Evening News
Mary Evans Picture Library
Cynthia Hollingworth
Manchester Libraries and Archives
Oldham Local Studies and Archives
Roger Morton
Messenger Newspapers
Peak District National Park Authority
Pat Reid
Harry Rothman
Stockport Archives
Marian Thilo
Rita Tilney
Tom Waghorn
Judith Warrender
Ian Watson
Working Class Movement Library, Salford

With special thanks to Roly Smith for his untiring and valuable assistance

Further information

Publications

On Foot in the Peak by Patrick Monkhouse (Alexander Maclehose, 1932)

The Untutored Townsman's Invasion of the Countryside by CEM Joad (Faber & Faber, 1946)

High Peak: The Story of Walking and Climbing in the Peak District by Eric Byne and Geoffrey Sutton (Secker & Warburg, 1966)

The Battle for Kinder Scout by Dave Cook (article in Marxism Today, August 1977)

First and Last: The Peak National Park by Roland Smith (Peak Park Joint Planning Board, 1978)

High Peak: Faces & Places by Keith Warrender (self-published, 1978)

Freedom to Roam: The Struggle for Access to Britain's Moors and Mountains by Howard Hill (Moorland Publishing, 1980)

The 1932 Kinder Trespass by Benny Rothman (Willow Publishing, 1982)

Kinder Log by T Nelthorpe (Cicerone Press 1987)

The Peak National Park: Official Guide by Roland Smith (Webb & Bower/Countryside Commission, 1987)

Forbidden Land: The Struggle for Access to Mountain and Moorland by Tom Stephenson (Manchester University Press, 1989)

Journeyman: An autobiography by Ewan MacColl (Sidgwick & Jackson, 1990)

Freedom to Roam by Harold Sculthorpe (Freedom Press, 1993)

The Peak District National Park: Official Guide by Roly Smith (Pevensey Press, 2000)

Wanderlust: A History of Walking by Rebecca Solnit (Verso, 2001)

The Essential Ewan MacColl Songbook compiled by Peggy Seeger (Oak Publications, 2001)

Kinder Scout: Portrait of a Mountain edited by Roly Smith (Derbyshire County Council, 2002)

Kinder Scout Mass Trespass: 70th Anniversary Celebration Souvenir Programme edited by Roly Smith (2002)

Trespass Trail by Martin Doughty & Roly Smith (2007)

Class Act: The Cultural & Political Life of Ewan MacColl by Ben Harker (Pluto Press, 2007)

Walk! A Celebration of Striding Out by Colin Speakman (Great Northern Books, 2011)

Websites

www.kindertrespass.com

Guardian report of the Trespass - www.guardian.co.uk/1932/apr/25/1

Working Class Movement library archives - www.wcml.org.uk/

Guardian Benny Rothman obituary - www. guardian.co.uk/news/2002/jan/25/guardian obituaries

Tribute to the trespassers with a poem by Derek Ward carved on a seat at Bowden Bridge quarry